THIRD EDITION

JAZZ ENGLISH

Real Conversations
Real Improvement

2

WORKBOOK
&
SOLO PRACTICE

GUNTHER BREAUX
With Chris Kobylinski

JAZZ ENGLISH 2 Third Edition
Student Workbook and Solo Practice

Gunther Breaux with Chris Kobylinski

2015 Compass Publishing

Acquisitions Editor: Peggy Anderson
Editor: Daniel Deacon
Design and layout: Gunther Breaux

http://www.compasspub.com
email: info@compasspub.com

ISBN: 978-89-6697-861-8

11 10 9 8 7 6 5 4 3
22 21 20 19

I would like to express my gratitude to Chris Kobylinski for his writing and content contribution. His knowledge of American and Korean culture makes this book more interesting, authentic and relevant.

Daniel Deacon's contribution as editor includes much more than editing. His visual and artistic sense, insight, and teaching experience have enhanced this book.

Website: jazzenglish.com

Printed in Korea

CONTENTS

All human learning can be summed up in three words:

Watch, try, repeat.

Here is where you repeat.
The more you repeat, the more you improve.

PREVIEW

Why use what's in *JAZZ* only once?

This workbook repeats and recycles what's in the main book. Just as in a workout, you use the same muscles in different exercises. You are going to use certain pages in *Jazz* in several different ways.

Variety. And repetition.

Save a tree. Repeat. Recycle. Improve.

Saying the same thing another way:

How do you get good at something?
You do it more than once.

This workbook uses what's in the book again. And again.

Spend less, improve more.

And save a tree.

Each unit has six pages.

1

LECTURE NOTES

This is great information, but there is just not enough time to cover it in class.

Explanations are provided for words that can be used in several ways (*diet, relax, bargain, hassle*), and on words that Koreans often misuse (*fun / funny; variety / various; boring / bored*).

Background and details for cultural differences for some of the Vocabulary Vitamins and Cultural Differences are provided. For example, I explain one of my favorite idioms. Do you know where *cut to the chase* comes from? Movies.

2

LISTENING & PRONOUNCING

This is a fill-in-the-blank activity using the Model Conversation on the third page of each *Jazz* unit. You listen and fill in the blanks, and then listen and repeat several times. You can then check the correct answers in the student book.

Many of the blanks are Vocabulary Vitamins. Listening to and writing down the new vocabulary helps you master it.

---

1 ALL ABOUT ME
LECTURE NOTES

What do you do? = *What is your job?* And further, what exactly do you do in that job?
For example: "What do you do?" " "I'm in banking."
Well, are you a bank teller or a bank president? Americans do not just answer with: *I'm a businessman.* ("Salaryman" is Konglish, so Americans never use that word.)
"What do you do?" "I'm a bank teller at the Kookmin Bank in Suyo-dong."
"What does your father do?"
"He's in the automobile business. He works for Kia in the human resources department."

In America, a hobby is an active activity, not something passive.
For example, watching movies and listening to music are not considered hobbies. Surfing the Internet is not a hobby. That is goofing off. On the other hand, if someone asks if you have a hobby, you could say:
I don't have a hobby, but my favorite pastime is reading a book / watching old movies / surfing the Internet / watching sports on TV / doing crossword puzzles.
Here is a definition: A hobby is something that you could be paid for doing if you were very good at it. If you were very good at playing tennis, playing the piano, sewing, or photography, you might be able to make money at it. If you are good at restoring antique furniture, you might eventually be able to start a furniture restoration business.

Is your whole family talented? Yes, my whole family is pretty musical. My family is musically talented.
Another way of saying that is: *Musical ability runs in my family.*
This is a common expression that is used for both good and bad qualities. For example:
Breast cancer runs in our family. Being overweight runs in the family.

personal space This is perhaps the first and biggest cultural difference that Americans notice in Korea. When waiting for a subway, an American will usually stand as far away as possible from another person, and will sit as far away as possible in the subway car.
Sometimes a Korean will move out of the way to let an American pass (for example, by the mailboxes in an apartment complex), and sometimes Koreans will not move aside because they think that there is enough room for a person to pass.
Just by observing, an American can often tell if a Korean has lived in America. Koreans who have lived in America give Americans more personal space.

physical with their friends Koreans have a Konglish term: *skinship*. This terms is confusing for Americans and difficult to translate. There is no corresponding phrase in English. The closest translation might be *physically affectionate*. It refers to a physically friendly—but non-sexual—friendship. It could be with same-sex friends, between boyfriend and girlfriend, or between husband and wife.

two-faced personality This means having two sides to your personality, like Jekyll and Hyde (from the Robert Louis Stevenson story).
The phrase is used to describe a person whose personality changes dramatically. For example, someone might normally be quiet and shy but become very outgoing when they drink or go to a singing room. Educated Koreans sometimes use the word *Janus* (from Roman mythology) to describe this concept.

8　　　1 ALL ABOUT ME

LISTENING & PRONOUNCING　1

1. Play the Model Conversation several times and fill in the blanks.
2. To check your answers, listen to the audio file again.
3. To improve, listen again, pronounce, and record yourself. Then listen to yourself. If you don't like listening to yourself, how do you think other people feel?

🎧 10

Brad　Hi. My name is Brad Kim.

Britney　Hi. My name is Britney Lee. Nice to meet you.

Brad　Nice to meet you too. Say, do you have a _____?

Britney　No. Why do you ask?

Brad　You look familiar, that's all. _____ had a class with a girl who looks just like you.

Britney　_____? Well, I have a lot of first _____, but none of them go to this school. Was she as pretty as me?

Brad　Oh, no. You are much . What's _____ than her.

Britney　Thank you so much. _____?

Brad　Diplomacy.

Britney　Ha. Now I get it. Do you always _____?

Brad　Only on the first day of class. Enjoy it while it lasts. What's _____?

Britney　Acting. And that _was_ my twin sister!

Brad　Ah. _____. How is your sister doing?

Britney　I was kidding about my twin sister. Is that great acting or what?

Brad　_____. Are you basically an _____? I'm going to guess extravert.

Britney　Yes, I like _____ with people. What about you?

Brad　_____. I like hanging out with people, but I also like my time alone. People can bring joy to your life, but they can also bring problems.

Britney　_____. What did you do last summer?

Brad　I had a _____ at Family Mart. Actually, my twin brother and I took turns going to work.

Britney　You have a twin brother?

Brad　_____!

1 ALL ABOUT ME　　9

5

3

ARTICLES

Articles in the Longer & Smoother Speaking paragraph on the sixth page of each *Jazz* unit are blanked out. To find the correct answers, simply turn to that page of each unit.

PREPOSITIONS

Prepositions and duration words in the Conversation Starters are blanked out. To check your answers, go to the second and third pages of each *Jazz* unit. 3Q is the third question. 3A is the answer to the third question.

In the beginning, you will be guessing, but gradually your brain will recognize a pattern, and soon you will be answering more quickly and correctly.

4

VOCABULARY WORKOUT

This is a fill-in-the-blank activity. Many units also have a matching exercise. Then there is a listening quiz based on the Vocabulary Vitamins. Go to the website **jazzenglish.com** and download the audio files. Then listen as many times as needed.

The fill-in-the-blank answers are in the back of the book, and you can check the matching answers in your student book.

---

1 ARTICLES & PREPOSITIONS

1. Fill in the blanks with an ARTICLE (*a, an,* or *the*). Some blanks may need no answer. 🎙 11
2. Listen to the audio file and check your answers. Then listen again and repeat.

If I had to choose one, I would say that I'm _____ extravert. First, I'm _____ joiner. I belong to two clubs: one in my major, and one outside of _____ university. The club in my major is _____ computer graphics club. We're learning how to make _____ webpage. We meet once _____ week, and well, sometimes we do more socializing than designing. _____ other club is a volunteer group that visits _____ elderly every Sunday.

Second, I am _____ party animal and night owl. I like to party and stay out late. I am definitely not _____ morning person. I do my best to schedule all my classes in _____ afternoon. After class, I usually hang out with my friends near _____ campus. However, I'm not _____ big spender. I'm _____ social drinker. I can sip on one beer for an hour. I like _____ party atmosphere of being around _____ lot of people.

Third, I'm _____ outgoing, outdoor person. On _____ weekends, I'm always on the go. I'm never home. My favorite sports are team sports. For example, I play soccer and basketball. I tried jogging and rollerblading, but that was just too boring without _____ company of others. So yes, I'm _____ extravert.

3. Fill in the blanks with a PREPOSITION or a DURATION word. 🎙 8-9
   AGO AT DURING FOR IN ON SINCE TO WITH WHEN WHILE
4. Listen to the Conversation Starters and check your answers. Then listen and pronounce.

1. 2A I'm majoring _____ law.
2. 4A I hate to get up early _____ the morning. My curfew is 11 p.m. _____ the week.
3. 5A _____ the weekends, I like to relax and hang out with my friends.
4. 7Q Are you good _____ computers? What kind of phone do you have?
5. 8A I'm more like my mother _____ appearance, but more like my father _____ personality.
6. 9A Last weekend, I went shopping _____ new clothes for school. I'm going _____ a cool new look.
7. 12A I was born _____ Anyang, and we moved to Seoul _____ I was 10.
8. 13A I have a fifth-degree black belt _____ taekwondo. I belong to the club here _____ school.

10   **1 ALL ABOUT ME**

VOCABULARY WORKOUT 1

1. Fill in the blanks with a Vocabulary Vitamin from page 18.
2. Do the matching.

1. My brother's a(n) _____.
   He rarely goes to bed before 4 in the morning.

2. Last weekend, I was a(n) _____ _____.
   I watched TV for nine hours on Sunday.

3. My father has a(n) _____.
   He gets angry very quickly.

4. My mother is a(n) _____.
   She cleans my room twice a day.

5. Professor, you're too _____.
   That's the fourth time her grandmother died this semester.

6. It's only 7 o'clock. Stick around a while. Don't be a(n) _____.

7. I have a short _____. I can only study for thirty minutes before I need a break.

8. You _____ too much. Just pick a topic and write your paper.

9. I was a(n) _____ in high school, but in college I want to be more sociable now.

10. Since she got that scholarship and won the beauty pageant, she's been _____.

1	generous		bad cop	1
2	good cop	1	grouchy	2
3	gourmet		gullible	3
4	honest		junk-food junkie	4
5	joiner		loner	5
6	a lot of patience		procrastinate	6
7	modest		short fuse	7
8	neat freak		slob	8
9	perky		social drinker	9
10	skeptical		stingy	10
11	weekend warrior		stuck-up	11
12	well-prepared		tell white lies	12

3. Go to jazzenglish.com, listen to the short dialogs, and mark the best answer. Sometimes there are two good answers. Choose the best one. Then listen and pronounce.

	1	2	3	4	5	6	7	8	9	10
A	○	○	○	○	○	○	○	○	○	○
B	○	○	○	○	○	○	○	○	○	○
C	○	○	○	○	○	○	○	○	○	○
D	○	○	○	○	○	○	○	○	○	○

Articles	Vocabulary	TOTAL correct
14 /20	8 /10	41 /54

Prepositions	Listening Quiz	% correct
11 /14	8 /10	76

How many *Articles* did you get right? *Prepositions*? *Vocabulary*? *Listening quiz* questions? Write your scores on this page and then on page 38. This way, you can keep track of your improvement.

11   **1 ALL ABOUT ME**

Do you want to check your answers AND improve your listening at the same time?

Don't open the book; play the audio file to check your answers. Simple.

After you check and correct your answers, play the audio file again. Listen, pause, and pronounce. Then record yourself and save the files. At the end of the semester, you can listen to how you sounded at the beginning of the semester. If you don't like to listen to yourself, how do you think other people feel?

5 - 6

ACADEMIC CONVERSATIONS WITH SPECIFIC EXAMPLES

Here, *academic* means *persuasive*. It means trying to convince someone that something is right or wrong, good or bad. To persuade, you give evidence—in other words, specific details.

This activity is great.

1. It will clarify your thinking. You will be organizing your thoughts.
2. Your speaking will get longer and smoother.
3. It will improve your writing and your speaking at the same time.
4. It's a great TOEFL essay practice. These short paragraphs are actually essay outlines: 1, 2, 3.

Just follow the examples and give your own specific examples. It is about your life and your details.

AND

If you forget your textbook, you can use these two pages as conversation starters.

---

1 ACADEMIC CONVERSATIONS
For example? Because 1, 2, 3.

ACADEMIC FORMAT FOR CONVERSATION TOPICS
Academic format means persuasive. It means not just stating an opinion, but giving reasons for that opinion. It means trying to persuade the listener that something is good or bad, right or wrong, fun or boring.

SPECIFIC EXAMPLES: *To be persuasive, off er evidence—SPECIFIC DETAILS. At least two or three specific details. It is hard to argue with specific examples.*

CONVERSATION FORMAT	ACADEMIC FORMAT
1. Last weekend was awesome.	Last weekend was awesome because A, B, C.
2. My parents are too strict.	My parents are too strict because A, B, C.
3. Harvard, I am wonderful!	Harvard, you should accept me because A, B, C.
4. My favorite movie is Shrek.	Shrek is my favorite movie because A, B, C.
5. I will tell you about my major.	I chose business as my major because A, B, C.
6. I love TGIFs.	TGIFs is my favorite restaurant because A, B, C.
7. My hobby is aerobics.	I love aerobics because A, B, C.
8. Professor, raise my grade, please!	Professor, you should raise my grade because A, B, C.
9. I broke up with my boyfriend.	I broke up with my boyfriend because A, B, C, D, E, F.
10. Daddy, buy me an iPad!	Daddy, you should buy me an iPad because A, B, C.

Imagine this conversation.

Daughter: *Daddy, you are so handsome, smart, and talented!*
Daddy: *What do you want?*
Daughter: *Wonderful father, please buy me a new iPad.*
Daddy: *No.*
Daughter: *Father, you should buy me an iPad because:*
A: I can save money on books—about $300 every semester.
B: I can get better grades. I can study anywhere, and maybe I can get a scholarship.
C: I can use it to make presentations and brochures for your company.
Daddy: *Here's my credit card.*

The daughter used specific examples and made a persuasive argument.

> **This is a great task:** A: It will clarify your thinking. You will organize your thoughts.
> B: Your speaking will get longer and smoother.
> C: It will improve your writing and your speaking at the same time.

12   1 ALL ABOUT ME

---

1 SPECIFIC EXAMPLES

> 1. Read the sample answers and write your own. Try to use new vocabulary.
> 2. If you do not like the question, make up your own and answer it.
> 3. Give specific examples: names, dates, times, places, amounts, whatever.
> 4. Why don't you type the answers on a computer and tape them here? That's what A+ students do.

1. **Are you basically an introvert or an extravert?**
I'm definitely an introvert. First, I have always been shy. When I am in a large crowd, it just takes my energy away. Second, I hate having a group project. I prefer to do something on my own. Third, I prefer individual sports, like jogging. I'm not into team sports.

_____
_____
_____
_____

2. **Who is stricter, your father or mother?**
My father is definitely stricter. First, he's very strict about my curfew. I must be home by 9 during the week and by 11 on the weekends. Second, he is fanatic about my grades. If I get a B in any subject, even sports, he punishes me. Third, my father is kind of cheap, and my allowance is very small.

_____
_____
_____
_____

3. **Are you usually well-prepared, or do you procrastinate?**
Half and half. In my creative classes such as Media Communications, I am well-prepared. For example, for my last project I had an idea immediately and worked on it all week. It came out great. On the other hand, in my detail classes, like Business Administration, I procrastinate. Three times already this semester, I had to ask the professor for an extension because my homework was late.

_____
_____
_____
_____
_____

1 ALL ABOUT ME   13

In the back of the book, there is an answer key for the Vocabulary Workout
and for the crossword puzzles in the student book.

This is solo practice.

Do it yourself and check yourself. Improve yourself.

1 ALL ABOUT ME
LECTURE NOTES

What do you do? = *What is your job?* And further, what exactly do you do in that job?

For example: *"What do you do?" "I'm in banking."*

Well, are you a bank teller or a bank president? Americans do not just answer with: *I'm a businessman.* ("Salaryman" is Konglish, so Americans never use that word.)

"What do you do?" "I'm a bank teller at the Kookmin Bank in Suyo-dong."

"What does your father do?"

"He's in the automobile business. He works for Kia in the human resources department."

In America, a hobby is an active activity, not something passive.

For example, watching movies and listening to music are not considered hobbies. Surfing the Internet is not a hobby. That is goofing off. On the other hand, if someone asks if you have a hobby, you could say:

I don't have a hobby, but my favorite pastime is reading a book / watching old movies / surfing the Internet / watching sports on TV / doing crossword puzzles.

Here is a definition: A hobby is something that you could be paid for doing if you were very good at it. If you were very good at playing tennis, playing the piano, sewing, or photography, you might be able to make money at it. If you are good at restoring antique furniture, you might eventually be able to start a furniture restoration business.

Is your whole family talented? *Yes, my whole family is pretty musical. My family is musically talented.*

Another way of saying that is: *Musical ability runs in my family.*

This is a common expression that is used for both good and bad qualities. For example:

Breast cancer runs in our family. Being overweight runs in the family.

personal space This is perhaps the first and biggest cultural difference that Americans notice in Korea. When waiting for a subway, an American will usually stand as far away as possible from another person, and will sit as far away as possible in the subway car.

Sometimes a Korean will move out of the way to let an American pass (for example, by the mailboxes in an apartment complex), and sometimes Koreans will not move aside because they think that there is enough room for a person to pass.

Just by observing, an American can often tell if a Korean has lived in America. Koreans who have lived in America give Americans more personal space.

physical with their friends Koreans have a Konglish term: *skinship*. This term is confusing for Americans and difficult to translate. There is no corresponding phrase in English. The closest translation might be *physically affectionate*. It refers to a physically friendly—but non-sexual—friendship. It could be with same-sex friends, between boyfriend and girlfriend, or between husband and wife.

two-faced personality This means having two sides to your personality, like Jekyll and Hyde (from the Robert Louis Stevenson story).

The phrase is used to describe a person whose personality changes dramatically. For example, someone might normally be quiet and shy but become very outgoing when they drink or go to a singing room.

Educated Koreans sometimes use the word *Janus* (from Roman mythology) to describe this concept.

LISTENING & PRONOUNCING

 10

Brad *Hi. My name is Brad Kim.*

Britney *Hi. My name is Britney Lee. Nice to meet you.*

Brad *Nice to meet you, too. Say, do you have a _____ ?*

Britney *No. Why do you ask?*

Brad *You look familiar, that's all. _____ I had a class with a girl who looks just like you.*

Britney *_____? Well, I have a lot of first _____, but none of them go to this school. Was she as pretty as me?*

Brad *Oh, no. You are much. _____ than her.*

Britney *Thank you so much. What's _____?*

Brad *Diplomacy.*

Britney *Ha. Now I get it. Do you always _____?*

Brad *Only on the first day of class. Enjoy it while it lasts. What's _____?*

Britney *Acting. And that <u>was</u> my twin sister!*

Brad *Ah. _____. How is your sister doing?*

Britney *I was kidding about my twin sister. Is that great acting or what?*

Brad *_____. Are you basically an _____?
I'm going to guess extravert.*

Britney *Yes, I like _____ with people. What about you?*

Brad *_____. I like hanging out with people, but I also like my time alone. People can bring joy to your life, but they can also bring problems.*

Britney *_____. What did you do last summer?*

Brad *I had a _____ at Family Mart. Actually, my twin brother and I took turns going to work.*

Britney *You have a twin brother?*

Brad *_____!*

ARTICLES & PREPOSITIONS

If I had to choose one, I would say that I'm _____ extravert. First, I'm _____ joiner. I belong to two clubs: one in my major, and one outside of _____ university. The club in my major is _____ computer graphics club. We're learning how to make _____ webpage. We meet once _____ week, and well, sometimes we do more socializing than designing. _____ other club is a volunteer group that visits _____ elderly every Sunday.

Second, I am _____ party animal and night owl. I like to party and stay out late. I am definitely not _____ morning person. I do my best to schedule all my classes in _____ afternoon. After class, I usually hang out with my friends near _____ campus. However, I'm not _____ big spender. I'm _____ social drinker. I can sip on one beer for an hour. I like _____ party atmosphere of being around _____ lot of people.

Third, I'm _____ outgoing, outdoor person. On _____ weekends, I'm always on the go. I'm never home. My favorite sports are team sports. For example, I play soccer and basketball. I tried jogging and rollerblading, but that was just too boring without _____ company of others. So yes, I'm _____ extravert.

1. 2A   I'm majoring _____ law.

2. 4A   I hate to get up early _____ the morning. My curfew is 11 p.m. _____ the week.

3. 5A   _____ the weekends, I like to relax and hang out with my friends.

4. 7Q   Are you good _____ computers? What kind of phone do you have?

5. 8A   I'm more like my mother _____ appearance, but more like my father _____ personality.

6. 9A   Last weekend, I went shopping _____ new clothes for school. I'm going _____ a cool new look.

7. 12A   I was born _____ Anyang, and we moved to Seoul _____ I was 10.

8. 13A   I have a fifth-degree black belt _____ taekwondo. I belong to the club here _____ school.

VOCABULARY WORKOUT

> **1. Fill in the blanks with a Vocabulary Vitamin from page 18.**
>
> **2. Do the matching.**

1. My brother's a(n) _____.
   He rarely goes to bed before 4 in the morning.

2. Last weekend, I was a(n)
   _____.
   I watched TV for nine hours on Sunday.

3. My father has a(n) _____.
   He gets angry very quickly.

4. My mother is a(n) _____.
   She cleans my room twice a day.

1	generous		bad cop	1
2	good cop	1	grouchy	2
3	gourmet		gullible	3
4	honest		junk-food junkie	4
5	joiner		loner	5
6	a lot of patience		procrastinate	6
7	modest		short fuse	7
8	neat freak		slob	8
9	perky		social drinker	9
10	skeptical		stingy	10
11	weekend warrior		stuck-up	11
12	well-prepared		tell white lies	12

5. Professor, you're too _____.
   That's the fourth time her grandmother died this semester.

6. It's only 7 o'clock. Stick around a while. Don't be a(n) _____.

7. I have a short _____. I can only study for thirty minutes before I need a break.

8. You _____ too much. Just pick a topic and write your paper.

9. I was a(n) _____ in high school, but in college I want to be more sociable now.

10. Since she got that scholarship and won the beauty pageant, she's been _____.

> **3. Go to jazzenglish.com, listen to the short dialogs, and mark the best answer. Sometimes there are two good answers. Choose the best one. Then listen and pronounce.**

	1	2	3	4	5	6	7	8	9	10
A	○	○	○	○	○	○	○	○	○	○
B	○	○	○	○	○	○	○	○	○	○
C	○	○	○	○	○	○	○	○	○	○
D	○	○	○	○	○	○	○	○	○	○

Articles	Vocabulary	TOTAL correct
14 /20	*8* /10	*41* /54
Prepositions	Listening Quiz	% correct
11 /14	*8* /10	*76*

How many *Articles* did you get right? *Prepositions*? *Vocabulary*? *Listening quiz* questions?
Write your scores on this page and then on page 58. This way, you can keep track of your improvement.

ACADEMIC CONVERSATIONS
For example? Because 1, 2, 3.

ACADEMIC FORMAT FOR CONVERSATION TOPICS

Academic format means *persuasive*. It means not just stating an opinion, but giving reasons for that opinion. It means trying to persuade the listener that something is good or bad, right or wrong, fun or boring.

SPECIFIC EXAMPLES: To be persuasive, off er evidence—SPECIFIC DETAILS. At least two or three specific details. It is hard to argue with specific examples.

CONVERSATION FORMAT	ACADEMIC FORMAT
1. *Last weekend was awesome.*	*Last weekend was awesome because A, B, C.*
2. *My parents are too strict.*	*My parents are too strict because A, B, C.*
3. *Harvard, I am wonderful!*	*Harvard, you should accept me because A, B, C.*
4. *My favorite movie is* Shrek.	Shrek *is my favorite movie because A, B, C.*
5. *I will tell you about my major.*	*I chose business as my major because A, B, C.*
6. *I love TGIFs.*	*TGIFs is my favorite restaurant because A, B, C.*
7. *My hobby is aerobics.*	*I love aerobics because A, B, C.*
8. *Professor, raise my grade, please!*	*Professor, you should raise my grade because A, B, C.*
9. *I broke up with my boyfriend.*	*I broke up with my boyfriend because A, B, C, D, E, F.*
10. *Daddy, buy me an iPad!*	*Daddy, you should buy me an iPad because A, B, C.*

Imagine this conversation.

Daughter: *Daddy, you are so handsome, smart, and talented!*

Daddy: *What do you want?*

Daughter: *Wonderful father, please buy me a new iPad.*

Daddy: *No.*

Daughter: *Father, you should buy me an iPad because:*
A: I can save money on books—about $300 every semester.
B: I can get better grades. I can study anywhere, and maybe I can get a scholarship.
C: I can use it to make presentations and brochures for your company.

Daddy: *Here's my credit card.*

The daughter used specific examples and made a persuasive argument.

This is a great task:	A:	It will clarify your thinking. You will organize your thoughts.
	B:	Your speaking will get longer and smoother.
	C:	It will improve your writing and your speaking at the same time.

SPECIFIC EXAMPLES

1. **Read the sample answers and write your own. Try to use new vocabulary.**
2. **If you do not like the question, make up your own and answer it.**
3. **Give specific examples: names, dates, times, places, amounts, whatever.**
4. **Why don't you type the answers on a computer and tape them here? That's what A+ students do.**

1. **Are you basically an introvert or an extravert?**

   I'm definitely an introvert. <u>First</u>, I have always been shy. When I am in a large crowd, it just takes my energy away. <u>Second</u>, I hate having a group project. I prefer to do something on my own. <u>Third</u>, I prefer individual sports, like jogging. I'm not into team sports.

   _____

   _____

   _____

   _____

2. **Who is stricter, your father or mother?**

   My father is definitely stricter. <u>First</u>, he's very <u>strict</u> about my curfew. I must be home by 9 during the week and by 11 on the weekends. <u>Second</u>, he is fanatic about my grades. If I get a B in any subject, even sports, he punishes me. <u>Third</u>, my father is kind of <u>cheap</u>, and my <u>allowance</u> is very small.

   _____

   _____

   _____

   _____

3. **Are you usually well-prepared, or do you procrastinate?**

   <u>Half and half</u>. In my creative classes such as Media Communications, I am well-prepared. For example, for my last project I had an idea immediately and worked on it all week. It came out great. <u>On the other hand</u>, in my detail classes, like Business Administration, I procrastinate. Three times already this semester, I had to ask the professor for an extension because my homework was late.

   _____

   _____

   _____

   _____

1 ALL ABOUT ME

2 WEEKENDS & NEIGHBORHOODS
LECTURE NOTES

What do you usually do on the weekends?

This is a very important question. Most people do pretty much the same thing every weekend. Your weekends are your leisure time. What you do in your leisure time kind of defines who you are.

What you usually do on the weekends is obviously important to you. If it is important to you, you should be able to describe it in detail: why you like it, how long you have done it, and how often you do it.

What weekend chore do you hate the most?

Just as what you love to do can help define you as a person, what you hate to do can also define you. If you hate to clean the house, you are probably not a neat freak.

Also, what someone likes to do, such as cooking, could be a chore for someone else.

Are you very skilled at something?

If you are skilled at something, the next obvious question is: How skilled are you? To answer this requires skills. For example: *I'm OK / so-so / fair / all right.* If you are very good at something, and you do not want to seem like you are bragging (자랑하다), you could preface your answer with something like: *I don't mean to brag, but I am pretty good at playing the piano.* Other phrases you could use are:

I don't mean to seem immodest, but I am a very good tennis player.

Actually, yes. I'm very good at drawing and painting. I've won several contests.

> **SKILL DEGREES**
> 1. *I'm bad.*
> 2. *I'm pretty bad.*
> 3. *I'm not too good.*
> 4. *Not really.*
> 5. *Sort of / kind of.*
> 6. *I'm not too bad.*
> 7. *I'm pretty good.*
> 8. *I'm good.*
> 9. *I'm very good.*
> 10. *I AM good!*

Do you ever entertain or have parties at your home?

Many Korean college students probably live at home, but most American college students do not. Many American college students have their own apartment, by themselves or with roommates. Therefore, it is more common for American college students and young adults to entertain at home.

This difference in where students and young adults live is reflected in dating habits. In Korea, most couples meet outside of the house. In America, no matter who lives where, the boy usually picks up the girl at her home, in his car.

CULTURAL DIFFERENCES

do-it-yourself Because an American home is typically a house and not an apartment in a complex, Americans are more likely to make their own minor home repairs. And they are more likely to make major repairs and even home additions, such as adding a bathroom or remodeling a kitchen. Because of this, there are many large do-it-yourself stores such as Home Depot and Lowe's. These large chains sell tools and building supplies to the public.

Cars used to be more mechanically simple, and many Americans could work on their own car. This is decreasing, but many Americans still do routine maintenance on their cars.

In America, it is much more common to have a house and a yard. Many Americans entertain in the yard with a cookout, or backyard barbecue. Cookouts are very common in the summertime or during holidays. Americans like to grill hamburgers, hotdogs, chicken, and steaks, although there are some personal and regional differences. The yards of households with children often contain swings and other playground equipment where neighborhood children gather.

LISTENING & PRONOUNCING

1. Play the Model Conversation several times and fill in the blanks.
2. To check your answers, listen again.
   To improve, listen again, pronounce, and record yourself. Then listen to yourself.

Brad   *Hey, Britney, how was your weekend? Did you do something special?*

Britney   *No. I just stayed home and _____. I was _____ from studying for the midterms.*

Brad   *Is that what all those tests were? _____?*

Britney   *_____?*

Brad   *Just kidding. I'm like you. I was _____ from all those tests. I'm really _____ to no tests for a while. Do you have any plans for this coming weekend?*

Britney   *Nothing special. I just hope to have some _____. My sister and I have been studying, and my father has been working late. So hopefully, we can all just _____ at home this weekend. What about you?*

Brad   *I have _____ to go phone shopping with Jack, but we're not exactly sure when or where yet. Frankly, I wouldn't mind just staying home and _____ for the whole weekend.*

Britney   *I know what you mean. By the time Sunday evening comes around, I start to _____ another week of school.*

Brad   *Well, let's do something different this weekend. Do you want to go white-water rafting?*

Britney   *This weekend? I'm not _____ like you. I _____.*

Brad   *Oh, come on. You can do it!*

Britney   *Thanks, _____. I would have to buy a whole new outfit. But if you're into water, there's a lake near my grandparents' house where we could rent a boat and paddle around.*

Brad   *You say <u>we</u> could paddle. You will paddle also?*

Britney   *Aw, come on, Brad. _____. <u>You</u> can paddle a small boat by yourself.*

Brad   *OK, but I don't want to paddle too fast for you. Maybe _____ some seasickness pills.*

Britney   *_____. I'll bring a whole bottle just in case.*

2 ARTICLES & PREPOSITIONS

> **1.** Fill in the blanks with an **ARTICLE** (*a, an,* or *the*). Some blanks may need no answer.
>
> **2.** Listen to the audio file and check your answers. Then listen again and repeat. 🎧 16

On Fridays after _____ school, I don't hang out around _____ campus; I hurry home. I live in _____ big high-rise complex in Incheon and there is lots to do near my house. My commute on _____ subway to school is about three hours each day, and by Friday night I am exhausted. Luckily, _____ complex is right next to _____ subway. My social life is mainly with my high school friends in my neighborhood. I haven't made any university friends yet.

Saturday is my big day. When I hear my mother start to clean _____ house, I play possum so she will not ask me to help. Then I surf _____ Internet and catch up on _____ news. I like to keep up with _____ latest movie and TV star gossip. Saturday evening I meet my friends, and we usually see _____ movie and then go to eat kalbi *or* haemul pajeon. *I have no curfew, but I usually get home before midnight.*

On Sunday morning, we go pick up my grandmother and go to _____ church. Then my dad takes us out to eat _____ Sunday brunch. Then it's back home, and I watch _____ TV for about six hours straight. If I've fallen behind on my schoolwork, I catch up on that late Sunday night. So on _____ weekends I get to hang out with my friends, have quality time with my family, and recharge my batteries for _____ next week of school.

> **3.** Fill in the blanks with a **PREPOSITION** or a **DURATION** word. 🎧 13-14
>   AT   DURING   FOR   FROM   IN   ON   SINCE   TO   WITH   UNTIL
>
> **4.** Listen to the Conversation Starters and check your answers. Then listen and pronounce.

1. 3Q   Do you use weekends to recharge your batteries or to catch up _____ schoolwork?

2. 6Q   Are you skilled _____ anything? Music, sports, art, science?

3. 9A   I live _____ Wangsimni, and that's near Hanyang University and the Han River.

4. 10A   I live _____ a high-rise with my older sister. It has a great view of Seoul Forest.

5. 11A   I wake up at 6 _____ the week and sleep till 10 _____ the weekends.

6. 12A   Last year he put a ceiling fan _____ every room _____ the apartment.

7. 15A   _____ weekends, I'm always _____ the go.

8. 16A   I party around school and take the last subway home _____ midnight.

VOCABULARY WORKOUT

1. **Fill in the blanks with a Vocabulary Vitamin from page 26.**

1. I had some _____ with my father last weekend. Usually, he's too busy.

2. Did you _____ in your neighborhood last weekend? I didn't see you around school.

3. My mother said she was _____ of me coming home after midnight.

4. Last weekend, I just stayed home and _____.

5. I goof off during the week, so I use the weekends to _____ my studies.

6. I have _____ to go meet my boyfriend, but he may have to work.

7. She's _____. Both of her boyfriends are in the army, and they met each other.

8. I said I'm sorry I forgot your birthday. Are you going to _____ all night?

9. My brother was a(n) _____ his first semester at college, but now he's focused on studying instead of drinking every Friday and Saturday night.

10. After midterm exams, I was _____ for a two weeks. It's like my brain stopped working.

2. **Go to jazzenglish.com, listen to the short dialogs, and mark the best answer. Sometimes there are two good answers. Choose the best one. Then listen and pronounce.**

	1	2	3	4	5	6	7	8	9	10
A	○	○	○	○	○	○	○	○	○	○
B	○	○	○	○	○	○	○	○	○	○
C	○	○	○	○	○	○	○	○	○	○
D	○	○	○	○	○	○	○	○	○	○

Articles	Vocabulary	TOTAL correct
14 /16	8 /10	40 /47
Prepositions	Listening Quiz	% correct
10 /11	8 /10	85

How many did **Articles** did you get right? **Prepositions**? **Vocabulary**? **Listening quiz** questions?
Write your scores on this page and then on page 58. This way, you can keep track of your improvement.

ACADEMIC CONVERSATIONS

1. Read the sample answers and write your own. Try to use new vocabulary.
2. If you do not like the question, make up your own and answer it.
3. Give specific examples: names, dates, times, places, amounts, whatever.
4. Why don't you type the answers on a computer and tape them here? That's what A+ students do.

1. **Do you use the weekends to recharge your batteries or to catch up on your studies?**
   Half and half. During vacations and when I'm not too busy, I like to recharge my batteries. I love staying at home and watching TV shows and relaxing. _On the other hand_, during the semester and especially before midterms and finals, I try to catch up on my studies. It's very important to get good grades, so I often spend my weekends catching up on my studies before big tests.

   _____

   _____

   _____

   _____

2. **On the weekends, are you a homebody or never home?**
   It depends. Sometimes I'm a homebody. When the weather is bad or when I'm really exhausted, I like to stay home all weekend, watch TV, and have some quality time with my family. However, when the weather is nice, I'm never home. I'm usually playing baseball or riding my bike along the Han River. In fact, I have two baseball games this weekend.

   _____

   _____

   _____

   _____

3. **Are you a party animal or a party pooper?**
   _I guess I'm a party animal. _First_, I'm very social. I love meeting and talking to people. _Second_, I love having a good time. During the week, I study, but I love to party on the weekends. _Third_, I love to drink. I don't drink a lot, but I enjoy having a few drinks. I think having a few drinks definitely turns me into a party animal.

   _____

   _____

   _____

   _____

SPECIFIC EXAMPLES

Because	For example	For instance	Also	Finally
Half and half.	It depends.	On the other hand		However

4. **Are you a weekend warrior or a social drinker?**

   Half and half. During the semesters, I am a weekend warrior. I live in the dormitory, and every Friday I meet my friends in my major and we have a club meeting. After that, we go to a beer hof and unwind. Sometimes, we skip the meeting and go straight to drinking. _On the other hand_, during the semester breaks, I hardly ever drink. My parents are Christian, and they frown on drinking. So when I live at home with them, I rarely drink.

   _____

   _____

   _____

   _____

5. **Are you spontaneous, or do you need advance notice?**

   It depends. When it comes to simple things, I'm pretty spontaneous. For example, I usually don't plan my weekends in advance. I just like to see what happens and go with the flow. However, when it comes to bigger things, like traveling, I need advance notice. I hate trying to go on a trip without planning. There are usually too many problems.

   _____

   _____

   _____

   _____

6. **Are you an indoors person or an outdoors person?**

   Half and half. During the week, I'm an outdoors person. I go to school and socialize with my friends near school. I'm in the soccer club, and we play once a week. _On the other hand_, on the weekends I'm an indoors person. I mainly stay home, watch TV, and hang out with the family. _Then again_, about once a month our family goes hiking in the mountains, so that is outdoors.

   _____

   _____

   _____

   _____

3 TECHNOLOGY

frugal, thrifty, cheap *Frugal* and *thrifty* are synonyms and mean that a person is very economical and doesn't like to waste money. People who are frugal or thrifty will try to save money by shopping around, looking for sales, or even making their own products. *Cheap* is similar, but it is has a negative connotation. Someone who is cheap doesn't like to spend money, and this attitude often affects others around them. For example, someone who is cheap will try to avoid paying their full portion of a bill or attempt to save money in extreme ways. If someone calls you "frugal" or "thrifty," it isn't a bad thing. If someone calls you "cheap," it is a bad thing. The word "cheap" can also be used as an adjective for an item or a store. If you say an item is cheap, it can mean that the item is of low quality or it has a very low price. In this case, cheap can be a good thing or a bad thing depending on the context. Usually, if someone says that a place is cheap, it means that the prices are low, so it's a good thing.

technophile, technophobe Both are good terms and are often used online. Terms that might be more appropriate for everyday conversations are *techie* or *tech-savvy* (the same as *technophile*) or *technologically challenged* (the same as *technophobe*). If your friend is really interested in computers and technology, you can say that your friend is a techie. If your grandfather can't figure out how to use his smart phone, you could say that he's technologically challenged.

GPS, black boxes GPS navigation units are becoming more popular in America, but black boxes are still not as common as in Korea. In fact, if you say *black box* in America, people will think that you are referring to the device that is in an airplane and won't know what you are talking about; you will have to explain what you mean.

remote control Don't use the term "remotcon" in English. Some people might guess what you are saying, but it isn't a standard English term.

selfie For many years, Koreans used the terms "selca" for a photo that someone took of themselves using a digital camera or phone. Until a few years ago, there wasn't a term for "selca" in English. Then the word *selfie* was created, and now it is commonly used and accepted.

SNS (social networking service) This is an English abbreviation, but it isn't commonly used in conversation. Most people will ask you whether you use a specific type of SNS rather than just asking if you use SNS. For example, someone might ask, "Do you have Facebook or use Twitter?"

CULTURAL DIFFERENCES

In general, Korea is a very high-tech country. Don't be surprised that many of the technological conveniences that you have in Korea aren't as common in America and other countries. In terms of phone networks, Korea has a very large high-speed network throughout the entire country. America is catching up, but some areas still have slow networks and poor coverage. Additionally, free Wi-Fi isn't as common in America as it is in Korea, and unlimited data plans aren't are not as common either.

In Korea and some other Asian countries, phone cameras make a noise when a photo is taken. This is a law, intended to prevent people from taking unwanted photos without others knowing. The US does not have such a law, so you might not hear a noise if you take a picture with an American phone.

LISTENING & PRONOUNCING

1. Play the Model Conversation several times and fill in the blanks.
2. To check your answers, listen again.
3. To improve, listen again, pronounce, and record yourself. Then listen to yourself.

 20

Brad   *Hey, Britney, _____?*

Britney   *I saw you yesterday, Brad.*

Brad   *_____. Ask me what's new with me.*

Britney   *OK. What's new with you, Brad?*

Brad   *_____ my new iPhone! I got it yesterday after school. It's _____.*

Britney   *_____. You mentioned something yesterday morning, but I didn't think you would buy one so quickly.*

Brad   *Oh, no. I'm an_____ kind of guy. I want it, and I want it now.*

Britney   *Lucky you. _____ did you get?*

Brad   *What's a data plan? _____! Check this out: Call Britney.*

Britney   *Well . . .*

Brad   *_____. I think it called my Aunt Britney in America. I hope I don't get charged. Anyway.*

Britney   *OK, easy question. How many _____?*

Brad   *Oh, I know, I know. Sixty-four. Well, I know how many I have, I'm still not sure what they are.*

Britney   *That's what I figured. _____?*

Brad   *I got it in Myeong-dong. The camera is _____. I think it is 10 or 12 megapixels. Whatever that is.*

Britney   *Have you taken any videos yet?*

Brad   *Yeah, I _____ on my Facebook page this morning.*

Britney   *Cool. Did you get any _____?*

Brad   *Like what?*

Britney   *One of those _____ that also carries your cash and credit cards*

              and _____.

Brad   *_____.*

Britney   *Did you get an arm strap for when you go jogging?*

Brad   *You think I am ever _____ on this baby? No way.*

Britney   *Sorry. Hey, let's take a _____.*

Brad   *OK, watch this. iPhone, take a photo! [click]*

Britney   *Neat. But I think you can just say "photo." [click]*

Brad   *Hey, you were right!*

ARTICLES & PREPOSITIONS

---

1. Fill in the blanks with an ARTICLE (*a, an,* or *the*). Some blanks may need no answer. 🎙 21

2. Listen to the audio file and check your answers. Then listen again and repeat.

My favorite device is my big 27-inch iMac. I just love _____ big screen. I also have _____ external monitor so I can write my essays on _____ Mac monitor and search for information on _____ Internet with _____ other monitor. This saves me _____ lot of time. And the Mac has a whole terabyte of memory, which is plenty to store all my videos. Also, I've started getting audio iBooks. I read them on _____ big screen and listen at _____ same time.

Second is my iPhone. Frankly, I don't use my phone much as _____ phone. I don't call people that much, and I certainly do not want to waste my time typing on a phone. In class, I set up my phone to record, and then when I get home, I can replay the professor's lecture. And sometimes I listen to _____ lectures on my subway ride home. I also like taking _____ photos and videos. _____ photos are good, and _____ videos are awesome.

Third, I like my iPad. I like reading, and I have _____ long subway ride every day to and from _____ school, so I read. _____ iPad is small enough to be portable and big enough so that it is not tiring on _____ eyes. And it is big enough that I can easily type emails and text messages. Phones are just too small for that. And _____ great thing is that all three devices easily talk to each other.

---

3. Fill in the blanks with a PREPOSITION or a DURATION word. Some blanks may need no answer.

    AT   **DURING**   **FOR**   **IN**   **ON**   **SINCE**   **TO**   **WHEN** 🎙 18-19

4. Listen to the Conversation Starters and check your answers. Then listen and pronounce.

---

1. 1A   It's awesome. I use it _____ texting and entertainment.

2. 2A   I have a big iMac desktop _____ home and a wireless printer.

3. 3Q   Who's better _____ technology, you or your father?

4. 4Q   Does your mother work? Do you call her _____ you'll be late?

5. 7Q   Do you belong _____ Facebook?

6. 11A   And _____ last summer break, I took a course _____ Photoshop.

7. 14Q   How often do you go _____ Facebook?

8. 16Q   Where will you go _____ shopping?

VOCABULARY WORKOUT

---

1. Fill in the blanks with a Vocabulary Vitamin from page 34.

1. For technology, my father is a(n) _____. He always buys the most expensive model.

2. Let me get this straight. A(n) _____ is for a computer, and a _____ is for a camera?

3. Bummer. My computer got a(n) _____ from some of that _____ I accidentally downloaded yesterday.

4. I'm a(n) _____ guy. I want it now, not later.

5. The sales guy said I would get unlimited data with the phone plan, but I was _____.

6. My sister is a(n) _____. She already bought seven phone cases because she liked all the colors.

7. Which _____ do you use, Google or Naver?

8. Besides Facebook, how many _____ are on your phone?

9. My father is too _____. He told me that I can get an old iPhone after the new one comes out.

10. Did you notice show good he looks in all his pictures? I think he's a(n) _____ expert.

---

2. Go to jazzenglish.com, listen to the short dialogs, and mark the best answer. Sometimes there are two good answers. Choose the best one. Then listen and pronounce.

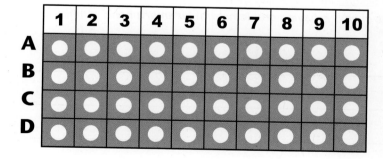

	1	2	3	4	5	6	7	8	9	10
A	○	○	○	○	○	○	○	○	○	○
B	○	○	○	○	○	○	○	○	○	○
C	○	○	○	○	○	○	○	○	○	○
D	○	○	○	○	○	○	○	○	○	○

Write your scores here and again on page 58.

Articles	Vocabulary	Total correct
/20	/12	/51
Prepositions	Listening Quiz	% correct
/9	/10	

ACADEMIC CONVERSATIONS

1. Read the sample answers and write your own. Try to use new vocabulary.
2. If you do not like the question, make up your own and answer it.
3. Give specific examples: names, dates, times, places, amounts, whatever.
4. Why don't you type the answers on a computer and tape them here? That's what A+ students do.

1. **Are you a bargain shopper or an impulse buyer?**
   I am a bargain shopper. <u>First</u>, I'm frugal and love getting a good deal. I'm always searching the Internet and stores for sales. <u>Second</u>, since I'm a college student, I don't have a lot of extra money. If I make a big impulse purchase, I'll have to eat ramyeon for a month. <u>Third</u>, I think I feel good when I save money. I never regret my purchases.

   _____

   _____

   _____

   _____

2. **Do you think technophile is a good thing or a bad thing?**
   <u>Half and half</u>. Technology makes almost everything we do possible, but it also causes problems. I use my smart phone to keep in contact with my family and friends back in my hometown, but it also causes me to waste time. I can also use my smart phone to do research, but I often just use it to search for cute cat pictures. Anything can be good if you use it or bad if you abuse it.

   _____

   _____

   _____

   _____

3. **Is your father a technophile or technophobe? What about your mother?**
   My father is a technophobe. <u>First</u>, he doesn't even know how to use the remote control properly. He is always asking how to turn up the volume. <u>Second</u>, he rarely uses our computer. He thinks it is just for email and checking sports scores. <u>Third</u>, he always is having problems with his smartphone. I think he only uses it to call me to ask how to use it.

   _____

   _____

   _____

   _____

SPECIFIC EXAMPLES

Because	For example	For instance	Also	Finally
Half and half.	It depends.	On the other hand		However

4.   In general, are you skeptical or gullible?

I'm very skeptical. I don't really believe anyone or anything. <u>First</u>, I think the media always lie to us. I think the news is about ratings and not about providing us with information. <u>Second</u>, I don't really trust companies. They always say their products are great, but often they aren't. <u>Third</u>, I don't trust the government. I think they're probably spying on me now.

_____

_____

_____

_____

5.   Is your father cheap or a big spender? Is your mother thrifty or really cheap?

My father is a big spender. He always spends a lot of money on his hobbies. <u>First</u>, he loves fishing and last year he bought a boat. My mother wanted to kill him. <u>Second</u>, he likes golf and always buys a new driver every year. <u>Third</u>, he just took up hiking, and he bought all kinds of camping gear and the world's fanciest tent. The tent has a remote control sunroof! I'm worried that he's going to try to buy a mountain.

_____

_____

_____

_____

6.   Do you use your phone more to talk or to text?

<u>It depends</u>. When I talk to my family, I usually call them and talk. I miss my family, so it's nice to hear them and talk to them for long periods of time. <u>However</u>, when I talk to my friends, I prefer to text. It's much quicker and easier. Plus, it's free and it's easier to text than to call while I'm in class. Of course, I rarely do that in class.

_____

_____

_____

_____

4 DATING & NIGHTLIFE

DATING LECTURE NOTES

CULTURAL DIFFERENCES

Valentine's Day, White Day In America, Valentine's Day is for both men and women, and the majority of giving is done by men. Korea has Valentine's Day, when the woman gives to the man, and White Day, when the man gives to the woman.

Who pays?

This does not describe every situation, but who pays goes something like this.
a) If the woman lets the man pay, maybe she likes him a little (or it could be that she is cheap).
b) If the woman insists on paying half, she maybe does not like him (or she is really into equality).

Double dates

American couples often go on a double date. That is when two couples go out together. This is usually two pairs of boyfriend and girlfriend. However, it could also be a boyfriend and girlfriend who are playing matchmaker for their friends, and the other couple is on a blind date. The blind-date couple feel better because their friends are on the date also.

Also, some shy girls might feel safer on a double date because there are more people around, and they might feel insecure being alone with a boy that they do not know too well. A double date is convenient for a couple on their first date. They are probably a little nervous and may have trouble finding something to talk about, so the other couple can help keep the conversation going.

DRINKING LECTURE NOTES

The more the merrier. "Merry" means happy. Some people like to go out with only one friend. Some people like to go out in larger groups. The larger the group, the better. The more, the merrier. = The more people we have, the more fun we will have.

Cannot remember Koreans have a great expression: *cut the film*. This is Konglish that describes when your brain's "camera" runs out of film and no more "video" is recorded.
Americans have no similar expression. Americans express the same concept like this:
I don't remember going there. My memory stops at about 2 a.m. Everything is black / blank after midnight. I don't remember anything after midnight. My mind is a blank after we left the nightclub. I blacked out.

Drinking without eating

Typically, when Koreans are drinking in a beer hoff, they order a side dish. If they order some more drinks, they order another side dish. As long as they are drinking, they order side dishes. If there is alcohol on the table, there is food on the table.

On the other hand, Americans do not necessarily order any more food. They might just keep drinking. And drinking.

In American bars, it is possible to order side dishes such as nachos, fries, wings, or other small appetizers, or even a meal like a hamburger, but it isn't mandatory. It is very common to drink at a bar in America and not order any food. A popular American bar food is chicken wings. These wings are very small and often come in a variety of sauces ranging from sweet to extremely spicy. If you like spicy chicken, order some hot wings.

LISTENING & PRONOUNCING

1. Play the Model Conversation several times and fill in the blanks.
2. To check your answers, listen again.
3. To improve, listen again, pronounce, and record yourself. Then listen to yourself.

Brad   *Hey, Britney, who was that _____ that I saw you with at the library?*

Britney   *Oh, that was Bob Taylor.*

Brad   *Is he your _____?*

Britney   *No, he's _____. I've known him since elementary school.*

Brad   *Come on, you two looked pretty chummy. I thought I saw sparks.*

Britney   *_____. His girlfriend is studying in America, and I just keep him company. Free meals for me, and he doesn't get bored sitting at home all the time. Say, how was your _____ last weekend?*

Brad   *She had a _____.*

Britney   *Ouch. OK, besides not being beautiful, what was wrong with her?*

Brad   *Aw, she was OK, I guess. She just _____.*

Britney   *What is your type? You're just too _____!*

Brad   *I'm not picky. I just have high standards. I'm saving myself for _____.*

Britney   *Yeah, right. Tell me about it. You're not going to meet Miss Right in a bar, you know.*

Brad   *_____. Besides, I'm too shy to talk to women without alcohol.*

Britney   *No, you're _____. You're only concerned with their looks. If they don't look like a cheerleader, you're not interested.*

Brad   *Say what? No. I'm a lonely, sensitive, caring guy.*

Britney   *Lonely? You're out with a different girl _____.*

Brad   *There, you see? That means that I'm lonely but looking very hard.*

Britney   *Yeah, right. And I'm Hyolyn.*

Brad   *And what about you? _____. You only had two dates with Jake, and then you wouldn't see him anymore.*

Britney   *He turned out to be a _____.*

Brad   *Yeah, but a rich nerd.*

Britney   *That's why I went on the second date. It was _____. Do you really think I'm going to break up with a rich guy BEFORE my birthday?*

Brad   *Oh, _____, Britney.*

4 ARTICLES & PREPOSITIONS

My Mr. Right will be tall and good-looking, but not too good-looking. I do not like _____ people who are vain. And if my boyfriend is really handsome, too many girls will flirt with him. _____ very good-looking mate can be _____ high-maintenance. I'd like somebody who is affectionate, but not affectionate in public. But I don't want _____ cold fish either. Of course, my ideal man must be faithful. And he must trust me. I don't like _____ jealous or possessive boyfriends. I believe in love at first sight because my father says that's what happened to him. He saw my mom in _____ restaurant near work and thought: I'm going to marry her. Mom says that story is not true, but dad swears it is. But they did have _____ whirlwind romance. They dated for only six months before getting married. Mom said she tried to play hard to get, but dad was just too cute. Her mom told her when she was _____ teenager: Find guys who make you laugh, and marry the best looking one.

Funny story: Mom says that one of the things she liked about dad was that he was not _____ heavy drinker. Actually, dad was _____ weekend warrior. He was just smart enough never to drink heavily around her. Some people told her that he drank, but she did not believe them until their _____ honeymoon. She said after she found out, she gave him _____ silent treatment for two hours, but then, like she always says, he's just too cute.

3. Fill in the blanks with a **PREPOSITION** or a **DURATION** word. 23-24
   AT   DURING   FOR   FROM   IN   ON   SINCE   TO   WITH   UNTIL
4. Listen to the Conversation Starters and check your answers. Then listen and pronounce.

1. 1A   My parents met _____ college.

2. 2A   I definitely believe _____ love _____ first sight.

3. 3A   My father is a doctor, so my mother's parents liked him _____ the start.

4. 5Q   Have you ever had a crush _____ someone?

5. 5A   I had a crush _____ this jock in high school. He was out of my league, but he was so cute.

6. 9A   Well, I had a boyfriend _____ last weekend.

7. 11A   I drink anything, and all beers taste the same _____ me.

8. 14A   The girls were pretty but not interested _____ us.

VOCABULARY WORKOUT

1. Fill in the blanks with a Vocabulary Vitamin from page 42.

2. Do the matching.

1. I just _____.
   I never actually spoke to her.

2. She _____. I waited for two
   hours, and no call, nothing.

3. He was my first _____. Oh,
   I was crazy about him when I was 13.

4. You're a(n) _____. If you can't
   be faithful now, what about later?

5. It was _____ for both of us.
   We were soul mates right from the start.

6. "I got a(n) _____ when I was
   in the army." "Bummer. Me too."

7. I was _____ when I saw my boyfriend kissing my best friend.

8. Don't be such a(n) _____. Stop pouting and get in the swing of things.

9. I was twenty minutes late, so she gave me _____ for two hours.

10. My date was a(n) _____. She drank only one beer and laughed all night long.

1	belle of the ball		cold fish, cold	1
2	binge drinker		femme fatale	2
3	early bird		high-maintenance	3
4	faithful		hold a grudge	4
5	forgive and forget		jealous; possessive	5
6	girl-next-door type		night owl	6
7	happy drunk		party pooper	7
8	life of the party		playgirl/playboy	8
9	high tolerance		low tolerance	9
10	low-maintenance		social drinker	10
11	party animal		teetotaler	11
12	touchy-feely		unhappy drunk	12
13	trusting		wallflower	13
14	weekend warrior		wet blanket	14

3. Go to jazzenglish.com, listen to the short dialogs, and mark the best answer. Sometimes there are two good answers. Choose the best one. Then listen and pronounce.

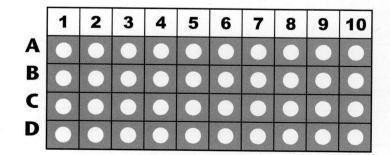

Write your scores here and again on page 58.

Articles	Vocabulary	Total correct
/12	/10	/44
Prepositions	Listening Quiz	% correct
/12	/10	

ACADEMIC CONVERSATIONS

1. Read the sample answers and write your own. Try to use new vocabulary.
2. If you do not like the question, make up your own and answer it.
3. Give specific examples: names, dates, times, places, amounts, whatever.
4. Why don't you type the answers on a computer and tape them here? That's what A+ students do.

1. **Are you an early bird or a night owl?**
   Half and half. I know that the early bird catches the worm, so I try to be an early bird. During the semester, I always try to get up early so I can catch the news and exercise before class. However, during vacation, I'm a night owl. I'm often up late. I usually like to go out and meet friends after I finish my part-time job, and often I don't go to bed until after 2 a.m.

   _____

   _____

   _____

   _____

2. **Do you believe in love at first sight?**
   Absolutely. First, I think physical attraction is very important. You would never date or marry someone that you are not attracted to, and you can see their looks at first sight. Second, of course, they might not love you back, but still, you are in love. Third, I think you can tell a lot from the first impression: how they dress, how they speak (educated or crude), how often they smile, how they treat other people.

   _____

   _____

   _____

   _____

3. **Is your boyfriend or girlfriend high-maintenance or low-maintenance?**
   Sadly, my boyfriend is high-maintenance. <u>First</u>, he acts like he's in a boy band. He spends so much time doing his hair and getting ready. <u>Second</u>, he always has to eat at trendy restaurants. He's always reading blogs to find out the coolest places to eat. <u>Third</u>, he's really sensitive. If I criticize him, he gets ticked off. I think I'll break up with him. After all, boyfriends are like buses: another one will be along in ten minutes.

   _____

   _____

   _____

   _____

SPECIFIC EXAMPLES

Because	For example	For instance	Also	Finally
Half and half.	It depends.	On the other hand		However

4. **Are you a material girl or a spiritual girl? Is your girlfriend a *femme fatale* or the girl-next-door type?**
I'm definitely a material girl. <u>First,</u> I love shopping. It is my favorite thing to do. <u>Second,</u> I love drinking coffee. I'm a VIP at most coffee shops near school. <u>Third,</u> I always have to have the newest tech. I can't wait till the new iPhone comes out. I'm living in a material world, so I have to be a material girl. It's my job to help the economy. In fact, it's my patriotic duty to spend money.

_____

_____

_____

_____

5. **Are you a weekend warrior or a social drinker? A binge drinker or a teetotaler?**
I'm definitely a social drinker. <u>First,</u> I don't have a high tolerance. If I drink too much, I get very drunk and sick. <u>Second,</u> I hate having a hangover. I think weekend warriors waste their whole weekend. They spend the nights drinking and the days recovering. <u>Third,</u> I think it is important to drink responsibly. I hate when people do stupid things when they are drunk.

_____

_____

_____

_____

6. **Are you a happy drunk or an unhappy drunk?**
<u>It depends</u> on what I'm drinking. If I drink beer, soju, or cocktails, I'm a happy drunk. I become the life of the party, and I have a great time. However, if I drink wine, I become very unhappy. I start to think about problems and become a wet blanket. And, if I drink tequila, look out. I get a little crazy. And, oh, when I drink vodka, whoa, I get really crazy. Once, I ended up in a park, talking to a statue.

_____

_____

_____

_____

5 SOFA TIME:
TV, MUSIC, & READING

LECTURE NOTES

AMERICA'S TV AND MOVIE CULTURE

Do you watch American movies and TV? Even if you understood every word they said, you would very often not know that they meant. Why? Because when Americans speak, they use movies and TV shows, and characters in those movies and shows, to describe things. And if you don't know a lot about American movies, TV shows, and their characters, you will not understand what they are talking about.

Have you heard the saying: A picture is worth a thousand words? Well, referring to a movie, TV show, book, or song is worth a hundred words. It allows the writer to give a lot of information with very few words.

Did you see *Miss Congeniality* with Sandra Bullock? She plays an FBI agent pretending to be a beauty contestant. She is not the delicate, feminine type. She is rather manly and forceful. Michael Caine (the butler in *Batman*) is her beauty coach. He usually works with beauty contest winners, not FBI agents. Finally, he is exasperated (을 화나게 하여 자포자기하게 하다) and says: *The other coaches have Rose Bowl Queens and I've got Dirty Harriet.*

Who the heck is Dirty Harriet? Caine is referring to a movie character. *Dirty Harry* is a Clint Eastwood police detective movie. Clint Eastwood played a macho, violent, tough-guy detective. He beats up and shoots bad guys. (This was an influential movie because it created a new genre of violent, good-guy movies.) Thus, even if you clearly understood that Michael Caine said "Dirty Harriet," unless you knew a lot about American movies, you would have no idea what he meant. If you know American TV, movies, and music, you will know what they're talking about.

comedians, talents, celebrities Koreans often use the word "talent" for a person who is on TV a lot. (Personally, I do not often know what their particular talent is. Some appear to only have a weird hairdo.) Americans use the word "celebrity" for people like this. Paris Hilton is a celebrity (again, I'm not sure what her talent is). Therefore, instead of using the word "talent," use the word "celebrity," and an American will know what you are talking about.

Do you play a musical instrument? This is not a very common question in America, and most people would answer: No, why do you ask? However, in Korea, the odds are pretty good that someone, especially a woman, would answer "yes" to this question.

CULTURAL DIFFERENCES

prime time This is between 7 and 10 p.m. It is called prime time because this is when most people are watching TV, and thus, this is when most people will see the advertising (TV commercials). The more people that watch a certain TV program, the more the TV company can charge for commercials.

Where does the name *soap opera* come from? In the early days of radio, many radio shows were dramas. And many of the sponsors of those radio shows were soap detergent companies. (The sponsors paid for the show, so the commercials were all for the sponsor's products, soap.)

The shows were often a little bit overly dramatic, so they were jokingly referred to as "operas." And the name for an overly dramatic show became "soap opera." *Soap opera* can refer to an overly dramatic TV show, and it can also be used to describe a stormy relationship. *She's getting divorced again? Her life is just one big soap opera.*

Britney	*Hi. Before we start talking about today's topic, _____?*
Brad	*Let's see. I watched TV. What about you?*
Britney	*I went to the _____ and prepared for this class. Well, what did you do last weekend?*
Brad	*I watched TV.*
Britney	*Really? Are you a professional _____? Is that all you do?*
Brad	*No, silly. I was preparing for this class. The topic is Sofa Time! TV time! I even _____.*
Britney	*Finally, a topic you're interested in.*
Brad	*_____. I'm a TV expert. I grew up on TV.*
Britney	*OK, let's have it. What did you watch?*
Brad	*Oh, I saw a new genre of TV show. It's a musical _____.*
Britney	*Really? Good research. Tell me more.*
Brad	*Yeah, it's based on a _____. Remember the movie Mamma Mia?*
Britney	*Sure. But I didn't know they made a _____ to Mamma Mia.*
Brad	*They did. It was called Grandmamma Mia.*
Britney	*_____.*
Brad	*What kind of shows do you like?*
Britney	*I like the _____ live music programs. I like the dancing and choreography.*
Brad	*I like them too, but I wish they would sing live _____.*
Britney	*True. And after one group has a hit song, there are a bunch of _____ groups imitating them.*
Brad	*Yeah, that happens a lot with the _____. Girl groups too.*
Britney	*What kind of shows do your parents watch?*
Brad	*My mom likes _____.*
Britney	*My mom too, but my father hates them. He likes _____.*
Brad	*Does your father read a lot?*
Britney	*A lot. He doesn't like _____. He mainly reads history. A lot of _____.*
Brad	*My mother reads a lot, but only _____.*
Britney	*_____?*
Brad	*Well, I don't remember the titles, but she's always asking my father, "Tell me again—why did I marry you?"*

ARTICLES & PREPOSITIONS

My favorite TV show is The Big Bang Theory. It's _____ American sitcom about three science nerds in Los Angeles and their relationships with _____ women. The show has several stereotypes: _____ dumb blond waitress trying to be _____ actress, _____ Jewish nerd who has _____ domineering mother, and _____ super-nerd who is so smart he has trouble understanding normal human emotions. There is also _____ Indian guy with _____ thick accent who is often puzzled by American culture.

My favorite singing group is Maroon 5. Their voices are just so harmonious. I saw them when they came to Seoul _____ few years ago. I really like _____ fact that they are talented enough to sing live. They don't lip-sync. They all have great voices, and they sing with such sincerity.

Also, I like to read _____ lot. I have over _____ hundred books, mainly history and biography. I never read fiction. Lately, I've been reading _____ lot on the Internet. After watching _____ movie or TV show, I'll go to _____ Internet and read all about it and _____ actors. My next project is to get _____ audiobooks and read them and listen at _____ same time. I want to find books that have _____ good vocabulary that I can learn.

3. Fill in the blanks with a **PREPOSITION** or a **DURATION** word. Some blanks may need no answer.
   OF   FROM   AT   DURING   FOR   IN   ON   SINCE   TO   WHEN   28-29
4. Listen to the Conversation Starters and check your answers. Then listen and pronounce.

1. 2A   Four hours _____ Saturday and about six _____ Sunday. I like TV.

2. 4A   I think most _____ the male singers are Rain wannabes—all the same.

3. 7Q   Do you read books _____ English?

4. 8A   I get my news mainly _____ TV, and I'll go _____ the Internet for background information.

5. 9A   I saw Lady Gaga when she came _____ Seoul. She was shorter than I thought.

6. 12Q   What is your favorite movie genre? What kind _____ movies do you hate?

7. 13A   I have lots of books _____ my iPad.

8. 15A   I went _____ a girl-group concert _____ Jamsil last year.

VOCABULARY WORKOUT

---

1. Fill in the blanks with a Vocabulary Vitamin from page 50.

1. The _____ from that movie were funnier than the movie.

2. There was a(n) _____ in that time travel movie, but I was so confused I missed it.

3. How can they make a(n) _____ to *The End of the World*?

4. Whoa! That scene was kind of sexy for _____.

5. I think _____ stories are bad for girls. It makes them think someone else can solve all their problems.

6. In the beginning, she was the _____. Then she lost twenty pounds, had plastic surgery, and became a(n) _____.

7. Now, that's what I call a(n) _____. I counted eight major stars in there.

8. He always plays the leading man's funny _____. He never plays the lead.

9. The stars were both good-looking and good actors, but they had no _____.

10. Your life is like a(n) _____! There's always some dramatic problem. You need to get your life in order.

---

2. Go to jazzenglish.com, listen to the short dialogs, and mark the best answer. Sometimes there are two good answers. Choose the best one. Then listen and pronounce.

	1	2	3	4	5	6	7	8	9	10
A	○	○	○	○	○	○	○	○	○	○
B	○	○	○	○	○	○	○	○	○	○
C	○	○	○	○	○	○	○	○	○	○
D	○	○	○	○	○	○	○	○	○	○

Write your scores here and again on page 58.

Articles	Vocabulary	Total correct
/19	/11	/51
Prepositions	Listening Quiz	% correct
/11	/10	

ACADEMIC CONVERSATIONS

1. Read the sample answers and write your own. Try to use new vocabulary.
2. If you do not like the question, make up your own and answer it.
3. Give specific examples: names, dates, times, places, amounts, whatever.
4. Why don't you type the answers on a computer and tape them here? That's what A+ students do.

1. **What is your favorite TV show? Why?**

My favorite TV show is Game of Thrones. *I like it for many reasons. <u>First</u>, the story is amazing. The plot is so interesting, and there are many plot twists. <u>Second</u>, the characters are great. Each character is unique, and it is very easy to love or hate them. <u>Third</u>, the scenes are awesome. The quality is much better than most movies.*

_____

_____

_____

2. **Who is your favorite TV star or comedian? Why?**

My favorite comedian is Lee Hui-jae. I think many Koreans love him. <u>First</u>, he is very funny. He makes everyone laugh and really improves every show that he is on. <u>Second</u>, he is on many different shows. It is nice to see him interact with other comedians and famous people. <u>Third</u>, I really like that show he is on with his twin sons, Superman Came Back.

_____

_____

_____

3. **Who is your favorite singer or group? Why?**

My favorite group is Sistar. They are the best. <u>First</u>, their songs are very catchy. I really like to listen to all of their songs. I always listen to their songs when I'm on the subway. <u>Second</u>, I love their music videos. All of the videos have great dances. <u>Third</u>, I really like Hyolyn. She can sing! I heard her sing live once. Her voice is so pure. I think she could be a great solo act. She's also very photogenic.

_____

_____

_____

SPECIFIC EXAMPLES

| Because | For example | For instance | Also | Finally |
| Half and half. | It depends. | On the other hand | However |

4. What are your three favorite movies?

My three favorite movies are The Shawshank Redemption, Roaring Currents, *and* The Avengers. <u>*First*</u>, The Shawshank Redemption *is a classic buddy movie. I love watching it when it is on TV.* <u>*Second*</u>, Roaring Currents *is an amazing movie. The action is great and I love Choi Min-sik.* <u>*Third*</u>, The Avengers *is great. I love superhero movies, and this one has all my favorite characters.*

_____

_____

_____

_____

5. Where do you get your news—TV, newspaper, Internet, radio?

I usually prefer to get my news from the Internet. <u>*First*</u>, *it is very convenient. I can get the news 24/7 on my smartphone.* <u>*Second*</u>, *I can get the news on a wide variety of topics. It is easy to find international, local, and sports news on the Internet.* <u>*Last*</u>, *it is up to date. I can get the news as it happens on the Internet. That doesn't happen with a newspaper.*

_____

_____

_____

_____

6. Do you spend more time on your phone or on a computer?

<u>*Half and half*</u>. *I use my computer a lot for school and to watch movies and play games, but I chat, text, and play other games on my phone. I use my computer for typing papers and making presentations. I'm good at PowerPoint, and now I'm learning Prezi.*

_____

_____

_____

_____

6 HEALTH & FITNESS

LECTURE NOTES

cosmetic surgery, plastic surgery Cosmetic surgery is done for vanity, to improve appearance (like cosmetics). Plastic surgery is done for more serious purposes. If you have a nose operation to make you look better, it is cosmetic surgery. If you have a nose operation because of an injury, that is plastic surgery. While there is a difference, many Americans use the term *plastic surgery* for *cosmetic surgery* in conversations.

rehab (short for **rehabilitation**) If your leg were badly injured—for example, broken in several places--you would probably need rehab (rehabilitation). You would see a physical therapist once or several times a week. Soldiers who are severely injured in war are often in rehab for a long time.
> *I was in rehab for two months after my accident. = I went to rehab for two months after my accident.*
> *"How is your rehab going?" "OK. Slowly but surely. I can walk with a cane now."*

Rehab is also used for people with psychiatric problems, usually drug or alcohol problems.
When I found that my son was addicted to drugs, I put him in rehab for a month.

runs in the family *Are there any medical conditions that run in your family? Obesity runs in my family.*
Lung cancer runs in my family. The males in my family are prone to (likely to get) *heart disease.*

cold turkey To give up a bad habit cold turkey is to give it up immediately and totally.
> *I stopped cold turkey. I went cold turkey. I will stop cold turkey. = I will go cold turkey.*

dizzy, woozy

Dizzy is most commonly used for loss of balance, or equilibrium. For example, if you stand up and spin around ten times, when you finish you will be dizzy, or feel dizzy. *Dizzy* is NOT commonly used for how you feel before throwing up; that is nauseous. Before fainting, you might feel dizzy.

Woozy is used before you faint. And after you faint, as you are getting up.
She fainted, but she's up now. She's still a little woozy. Make her sit down.
If you are a really big Brad Pitt fan and you see him up close in person, you might feel a little woozy.

faint, pass out, black out All these terms mean to lose consciousness. However, "faint" has a kind of feminine connotation. "Black out" is more macho. "Pass out" is in between. In common usage: *She fainted. He blacked out. When his first child was born, he passed out in the delivery room when he saw all the blood. So the doctor would not let him in for the birth of his second child.*

cramps, bad time of the month The word *cramps* is generally used for women's monthly menstrual pain. So how would a woman politely decline an invitation (without going into details)? She would just say: *It's a bad time*. Or if speaking to someone she's close to, *It's a bad time of the month*.
> Jack: *Britney, I've got two free tickets to the Britney Spears concert. Let's go.*
> Nicole: *That's very nice of you, but no thanks.*
> Jack: *Say what? You love Britney Spears.*
> Nicole: *I know, but it's a bad time of the month. = It's a bad time. = It's not a good time.*

Of course, It's a bad time and It's not a good time do not always refer to menstrual cramps. Either of these expressions could mean that your mother is sick, or your father is angry, or your brother just got arrested, or something else that you do not want to go into detail about.

LISTENING & PRONOUNCING

 34

1. Play the Model Conversation several times and fill in the blanks.
2. Listen again, pronounce, and record yourself. And listen to yourself.

Brad   *Do you feel OK? You don't _____.*

Britney   *I feel terrible. I _____ all weekend.*

Brad   *Why don't you stay home?*

Britney   *No can do. My mother's _____ attendance.*

Brad   *My mom's the same way. I have to be half-dead to miss school. Do bad colds*
               _____?

Britney   *Yeah. We don't catch colds often, but when we do, they're bad.*

Brad   *Bummer. Do you _____ or stay home?*

Britney   *Oh, my father and brother want to go to the hospital. They moan and groan and think they're dying.*
               My mother and I are the _____.

Brad   *Funny. You, _____. I can't imagine.*

Britney   *_____. And after the cold season passes, we all have _____*
               from the _____ and dust.

Brad   *I can't imagine that. My family is always healthy. We don't _____, we eat and drink*
               \whatever we want, and never _____. Good genes.

Britney   *Lucky you. Well, what happened to you? Why is your arm _____?*

Brad   *Oh, I was rollerblading and tried something new.*

Britney   *And failed, _____.*

Brad   *Yeah. But a friend of mine took a video with his phone. Maybe I'll be famous on the Internet soon.*

Britney   *Dream on. What happened exactly? That looks like a _____.*

Brad   *Yes, it's turned several colors already. And my elbow was _____ yesterday*
               and last night, but the _____ this morning.

Britney   *Weren't you wearing a helmet and elbow and knee pads?*

Brad   *_____ don't wear those.*

Britney   *_____. Why don't you sit down? There's an empty seat.*

Brad   *I fell on my behind also. It hurts when I sit.*

ARTICLES & PREPOSITIONS

1. Fill in the blanks with an **ARTICLE** (*a, an,* or *the*). Some blanks may need no answer. 36
2. Listen to the audio file and check your answers. Then listen again and repeat.

I'm usually pretty healthy. I don't catch _____ colds often, but when I do, they're usually bad colds. Sometimes I have to go to _____ doctor and miss school. That happens about once _____ year, usually at _____ beginning of winter. I was in _____ car accident last year and got _____ cut on my head. I needed _____ stitches, but my hair hides _____ scar. That was _____ only time I have been to _____ emergency room in my life. That place was stressful. Since then, I've tried to stay healthy to avoid hospitals. About once _____ month I have _____ hangover, but I don't think that qualifies as _____ illness.

My parents believe in preventing illness rather than treating it. My mom fixes us healthy, well-balanced meals, and she gives us _____ spending money so that we eat right at _____ school and do not have to eat ramyeon or kimbap every day. My father used to jog all _____ time, but his knees now hurt him, so he swims or walks on _____ treadmill. My mom goes with him to _____ health club and does Pilates and yoga while he works out with _____ weights. I think _____ health club is kind of where they socialize. They go there for fitness and to meet their friends. And I guess having _____ good friends is good for your health also.

3. Fill in the blanks with a **PREPOSITION** or a **DURATION** word. 33-34

   AT   DURING   FOR   FROM   IN   OF   ON   SINCE   TO   UNTIL

4. Listen to the Conversation Starters and check your answers. Then listen and pronounce.

1. 1A   I broke my leg while snowboarding _____ middle school, and I missed a week of school.

2. 4Q   When you are sick or hurt, do you suffer _____ silence or complain a lot?

3. 5A   I fainted once _____ middle school. The sight _____ blood made me pass out.

4. 7A   Kind of. There was a gas leak _____ high school, and they evacuated the whole school.

5. 10Q   Did you like PE _____ high school?

6. 11A   I hate to exercise and love to pig out. Luckily, skinny genes run _____ my family.

7. 13Q   What sport would you like to be good _____?

8. 14Q   Are you allergic _____ anything?

VOCABULARY WORKOUT

---

1. Fill in the blanks with a Vocabulary Vitamin from page 58.

1. I _____ all over. I tripped and fell all the way down the stairs. I'm also _____ all over.

2. I played tennis for too long yesterday. My right elbow is _____.

3. I went hiking in the mountains yesterday and got a(n) _____. My skin is red and itches all over.

4. I had been watching TV for four hours, and then I stood up suddenly and I was _____.

5. It's _____ but not broken. The doctor said it was a bad _____.

6. Every year at this time, the _____ in the air makes my _____ act up.

7. When my little brother was born, my father stopped smoking _____. The bad news is that my brother is a teenager now and driving my father to drink.

8. Yuck, that smell is making me _____. Open a window and turn on the fan.

9. Oh, no! I have a blind date with a girl I have admired from afar, but I have this big _____ on the end of my nose.

10. She was drunk driving and got in an accident. So she's going to one _____ for her drinking and another for her injuries.

---

2. Go to jazzenglish.com, listen to the short dialogs, and mark the best answer. Sometimes there are two good answers. Choose the best one. Then listen and pronounce.

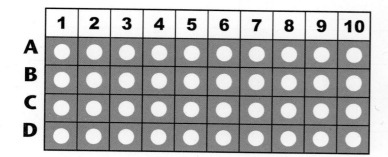

Write your scores here and again on page 58.

Articles	Vocabulary	Total correct
/21	/13	/54
Prepositions	Listening Quiz	% correct
/10	/10	

ACADEMIC CONVERSATIONS

1. **What is your favorite sport to play?**
   It depends. During the spring and summer, I love to play baseball. I belong to a team at my university, and we usually play other teams from our school. I play third base. _However_, during the winter it is too cold to play baseball, and I usually go snowboarding a few times every winter. I like snowboarding more than skiing because I think it takes more skill.

   _____

   _____

   _____

   _____

2. **What is your favorite sports team? Who is your favorite player?**
   _My favorite sports team is the LA Dodgers. _First_, baseball is my favorite sport, so I watch a lot of baseball. _Second_, I prefer to watch MLB. I also like to watch Korean baseball, but I really like MLB. _Third_, I like the Dodgers, because Ryu Han-jin plays for the Dodgers. He's my favorite, and I think he's the best pitcher._

   _____

   _____

   _____

   _____

3. **To get fit, would you prefer to eat less or exercise more? Why?**
   _I'd prefer to exercise more. _First_, I think exercising is more effective than dieting. I think dieting only gives temporary results. _Second_, I think exercising makes me feel better. I usually have more energy after I exercise. _Third_, I think exercising is better for my social life. I can exercise together with friends, but when I eat less, it's harder to go to dinner with people._

   _____

   _____

   _____

   _____

SPECIFIC EXAMPLES

| Because | For example | For instance | Also | Finally |
| Half and half. | It depends. | On the other hand | | However |

4. What is your favorite sport to watch?

My favorite sport to watch is soccer, specifically soccer during the World Cup. <u>First</u>, the World Cup is very exciting. All the teams are good, so the matches are fun to watch. <u>Second</u>, the World Cup involves the whole country. Since countries play other countries, the World Cup makes people feel patriotic. <u>Third</u>, the World Cup is very dramatic. If a team loses, they don't get another chance.

_____

_____

_____

_____

5. What three things do you do to stay healthy?

I do three things to stay healthy. <u>First</u>, I try to exercise every day. I run every morning. <u>Second</u>, I try to eat healthy. I try to avoid fast food and try not to eat late at night. <u>Third</u>, I try to get enough sleep every night. I think getting enough sleep is very important. I think these three things keep me healthy. Clean living, that's me. Unless I'm drinking, dancing, and gambling. Just kidding.

_____

_____

_____

_____

6. Do you think you should be able to buy medicine at a convenience store?

<u>It depends</u>. I think it is fine to buy basic medicine like aspirin and simple pain relievers at a convenience store. If someone has a headache or sore muscles, they should be able to get medicine for that easily. <u>On the other hand</u>, I don't think other types of medicine should be sold at a convenience store. If someone is sick, they should go to a doctor or a pharmacist, not GS25.

_____

_____

_____

_____

7 HOLIDAYS, FESTIVALS, & FEELINGS

burned out This means extremely exhausted because of work. It can be used for a short-term exhaustion or long-term exhaustion. For example, if you had a busy week at school, you might say, "I'm burned out; I need to rest this weekend." It can also be used to mean that someone has been overworked for a long period of time at their job and is no longer productive. For example, you might say that many people at that company work twelve hours a day and often burn out after about five years.

sick and tired This is an idiomatic expression that means that someone is angry about or tired of something that has been going on for a long time. So if someone says they are sick and tired of something, don't think that they are ill and exhausted. They are probably angry or upset.

envious, I envy you The phrase "I envy you" is overused in Korea. You might hear a native speaker say "I don't envy you!" if someone is in a bad situation, but you won't often hear them say "I envy you." There are better ways to express this idea. For example, if someone has a nice car, you can say something like "nice car," or "I wish I had a car like that," or "I'm jealous." In this case, "jealous" isn't a negative word.

Cultural Differences

Weddings: There are many differences between Korean and American weddings. First, in Korea, people aren't expected to RSVP to a wedding. If you get invited to an American wedding, you will be expected to RSVP, or they will assume you won't attend. This is because most American weddings have assigned seating and because they want to know how many people will be attending. Another difference is that in Korea, wedding photos are taken in advance and at the wedding. In America, photos are only taken on the wedding day. Additionally, in Korea, there is usually a wedding ceremony followed by a buffet or meal. In Korea, guests are expected to bring an envelope with money to the ceremony as a gift. In America, there is usually a wedding ceremony and later in the evening, there is a reception. During the reception, there is usually a meal, some speeches, and dancing and drinking. Most Americans will bring gifts or cards with money to the wedding reception.

Festivals: Themed festivals are becoming more popular in Korea. In America, there are many themed festivals, and there are also many cultural festivals because America is a multicultural society. Another type of event that many Americans region and states have is called a fair. Fairs are held in summer and usually last about a week. They feature rides, concerts, shows, competitions, and lots of food. These days, it is a trend that food vendors at fairs make very unique food items to sell. If you are curious, search the Internet and check out some of these interesting foods.

Halloween: Although Halloween is primarily a children's holiday, many university students and some adults in America wear costumes and attend Halloween parties. For children, Halloween is about wearing a costume and getting candy. Children usually go trick-or-treating. Trick-or-treating is when children put on their costumes and go to houses in their neighborhood and ask for candy. Adults usually wear costumes if they attend a Halloween party. For adults, Halloween isn't about candy; it's a fun social event.

Valentine's Day, White Day, and Black Day: Americans only celebrate Valentine's Day, and both men and women give their significant other cards and gifts. Chocolate is the most popular gift for Valentine's Day, but many men also give flowers. Sorry, single people—there is no Black Day in America.

Sporting Events and Games: Most sporting events are much more expensive in America than in Korea. In America, the average ticket price for a baseball game is almost $30.00, and the average price for a beer is more than $6.00.

LISTENING & PRONOUNCING

 40

1. Play the Model Conversation several times and fill in the blanks.
2. Listen again, pronounce, and record yourself. And listen to yourself.

Brad   Hey, Britney. How was your three-day weekend?

Britney   _____. We went to Everland.

Brad   I've been there. That place is _____.

Britney   Yeah. Well, originally, my father wanted a _____, but my sister and I got him to go for an exciting weekend.

Brad   Did your sister have fun too?

Britney   Eventually. We left early in the morning, and she is always _____ when she gets up early, so that was a pain.

Brad   How long was she _____?

Britney   Not long. As soon as she saw the entrance sign, she turned into a _____.

Brad   What was your favorite part of Everland?

Britney   Oh, the Tornado Roller Coaster. It'll _____. Talk about thrilling!

Brad   Did your mother ride it?

Britney   No way. She gets _____ on a glass elevator. But my sister screamed till tears came out of her eyes.

Brad   What about your father?

Britney   He's game for anything. He's _____. He was a paratrooper when he was in the army.

Brad   I wish my dad were the outdoors type. He just wants to _____ every weekend.

Britney   What did you do over the holidays?

Brad   Oh, I studied. My mother said she was _____ of my coming home late and low grades.

Britney   Ouch. So your mom is the _____?

Brad   Yeah. Frankly, I was kind of _____ when the holiday was over so I could come back to school.

Britney   You amaze me. Your dad didn't say anything?

Brad   No, he was asleep on the sofa. Or _____. He's pretty _____. Frankly, I think he's given on me.

Britney   You'll impress him some day. You're just a late bloomer.

Brad   _____?

Britney   Some flowers or plants start to grow late, but they end up OK.

Brad   Yeah, yeah, that's me. Bloomin' Brad! _____.

7 ARTICLES & PREPOSITIONS

> **1.** Fill in the blanks with an **ARTICLE** (*a, an,* or *the*). Some blanks may need no answer. 🎙 41
>
> **2.** Listen to the audio file and check your answers. Then listen again and repeat.

My favorite holiday is _____ Christmas because my parents are really into it. When I was young, my father would always dress up as Santa and come in _____ front door and give _____ presents, yelling, "Ho, ho, ho!" Of course, at _____ time I didn't know that was my dad. Mom is _____ great actress. She would act so surprised. My little sister would cry and scream in _____ fear, and I would just run straight to _____ presents. So I have great memories of Christmas.

My favorite festival is _____ Jindo Sea Parting Festival. That is just so neat the way _____ sea parts. I've been there four times, and it was awesome every time. We stay at _____ same place every time, and it has _____ great view. These days, it's getting commercialized and overcrowded. In France, there is _____ place called Mont St. Michel where _____ same thing happens. My dream is to go there.

My favorite birthday was last year. My birthday and high school graduation were on _____ same day, so I was one happy camper. We went out to eat with all my grandparents and took _____ bunch of pictures. That was _____ last time that I spent with all four of them, so those pictures are very special. They were all very proud that I got into _____ good university. And they all gave me money. Love and _____ soju flowed that night!

> **3.** Fill in the blanks with a **PREPOSITION** or a **DURATION** word. 🎙 38-39
>   AT   DURING   FOR   IN   OF   ON   SINCE   TO   UNTIL   WHEN
>
> **4.** Listen to the Conversation Starters and check your answers. Then listen and pronounce.

1.   1A   My birthday is _____ Christmas, so I get only half as many presents as my brother.

2.   2Q   Are birthdays big _____ your family? What did your parents give you _____ your last birthday?

3.   2A   My mom likes to bake and to take photos, so birthdays are perfect _____ her.

4.   3Q   What do your parents do _____ their anniversary?

5.   4Q   Does your mother drag you to weddings _____ distant cousins?

6.   6A   My father is big _____ going to the east coast to see the sunrise.

7.   7Q   Have you been _____ Nami Island? To the east coast for the sunrise?

8.   12Q   Did you get or give something _____ Valentine's Day?

VOCABULARY WORKOUT

1. Fill in the blanks with a Vocabulary Vitamin from page 66.

1. I'm _____ of having the lowest grade in all of my classes. I'm going to study—as soon as I find out where the library is.

2. A child at the table next to us had a(n) _____, and his parents did nothing. I'll never eat there again.

3. When I study, I listen to classical music—mainly Mozart. It's very _____ and helps me relax.

4. And then my blind date showed me the big pimple on his neck, and I was like, "_____!"

5. Please don't _____. How was I to know that was your twin sister?

6. I was _____ when I tripped and fell during the race.

7. I'm not _____ that she's so pretty. I'm _____ that she gets straight As without studying.

8. I was _____ when my sister dropped my new phone in the river. Someday, some way, I will get _____.

9. Every Sunday night, I get _____ about the coming week at school. I really need to do my homework before Monday morning.

10. That class bores me. It's so _____—just boring lectures all the time.

2. Go to jazzenglish.com, listen to the short dialogs, and mark the best answer. Sometimes there are two good answers. Choose the best one. Then listen and pronounce.

	1	2	3	4	5	6	7	8	9	10
A	○	○	○	○	○	○	○	○	○	○
B	○	○	○	○	○	○	○	○	○	○
C	○	○	○	○	○	○	○	○	○	○
D	○	○	○	○	○	○	○	○	○	○

Write your scores here and again on page 58.

Articles	Vocabulary	Total correct
/18	/13	/50
Prepositions	Listening Quiz	% correct
/9	/10	

> 1. Read the sample answers and write your own. Try to use new vocabulary.
> 2. If you do not like the question, make up your own and answer it.
> 3. Give specific examples: names, dates, times, places, amounts, whatever.
> 4. Why don't you type the answers on a computer and tape them here? That's what A+ students do.

1. What is your favorite theme park? Why?

My favorite theme park is Everland. <u>First</u>, Everland is close to Seoul. It's in Yongin, so I can take a bus there. <u>Second</u>, it has many fun rides. I really love the T Express. It's a great rollercoaster. <u>Third</u>, it's right next to Caribbean Bay. If I want to go to an amusement park and a water park, it is possible to do both in the same day.

_____

_____

_____

_____

2. What is your favorite holiday? Why?

My favorite holiday is Christmas. <u>First</u>, I love seeing all the Christmas decorations and lights. I like the way lights look on a snowy night. <u>Second</u>, I love getting and receiving presents. I love shopping for gifts and getting gifts from others. I really like it when I get more gifts than I give! <u>Third</u>, I love having the day off. It is great to have time off toward the end of a long year. Overall, I like the mood of the Christmas season.

_____

_____

_____

3. What is the best festival you have ever been to? Why?

The best festival that I have ever been to is the Yangyang Salmon Festival. <u>First</u>, it is held in the fall. Fall is my favorite season. <u>Second</u>, Yangyang is a very beautiful place. It is near the ocean and near Seoraksan, so there are many things to do besides the festival. <u>Third</u>, you get to catch a salmon with your bare hands. How cool is that?

_____

_____

_____

_____

SPECIFIC EXAMPLES

Because	For example	For instance	Also	Finally
Half and half.	It depends.	On the other hand		However

4. **What causes you stress? School? Parents? Friends? Commuting? Global warming? Why?**

It depends. During the semester, school and tests give me stress. It is very hard to keep up with all the work, and I get anxious about doing projects and presentations. I'm especially stressed during midterms and finals. On the other hand, during vacation, my parents cause me stress. They always ask me why I didn't get better grades and tell me to get a part-time job.

_____

_____

_____

_____

5. **What are your pet peeves (little things that make you angry)?**

I hate to wait, so my pet peeves all involve people being rude and making me wait. For example, I hate it when the person ahead of me at the ATM counts their money before leaving. Move! Also, I hate it when the person ahead of me in a grocery store has to dig in their purse to find the money to pay. Finally, I get ticked off when somebody takes a really long time using a public restroom. Other people need it, too!

_____

_____

_____

_____

6. **What was the best time in your whole life? Why?**

The best time in my life is now, my college years. First, I get to meet many new people. Every year, I meet new people and make new friends. Second, I finally get to study the classes that I want. I didn't have any choices in high school, but now I can choose some classes that I want to take. Third, I get to experience freedom. I'm living on my own and learning to become an adult. It is fun and exciting.

_____

_____

_____

_____

8 WORKING & GETTING THERE

perks This word is short for *perquisites*, which are benefits over and above regular income. For example, one of the perks of working for Samsung Electronics might be a free cell phone or notebook computer. One of the perks of working for Korean Airlines is that you get to fly at a big discount. A Hilton Hotel employee might get to stay at any Hilton worldwide at a reduced rate. Simply put, a perk is a freebie from the place you work. It could be a convenient parking spot or a good company cafeteria that charges very little.

CULTURAL DIFFERENCES

What do your parents do? This is a fairly common question when getting to know someone. A parent's job can often tell you quite a lot about a person very quickly. This question might be a bit personal in Korea, but it is not in America.

You are your car.

Cars are very important to Americans (especially males). The type of car you have lets the world know what kind of guy you are.

- If you have an old, beat-up car, you are obviously not very successful.
- If you have a shiny new BMW, Mercedes, or Porsche, you are obviously very successful (or your parents are).
- If you have a lot of money but a practical car, you are a practical person.

Are you practical, hip, cool, and successful, or just a lazy wannabe? They will immediately know as soon as you drive up.

On the other hand, a real man can drive anything, and everybody will still know that he is a real man. (Think Brad Pitt.) The more secure a man is in his identity and in his manliness, the less he needs a manly car. Therefore, in some cases, when a man has a really expensive car, some people think: *What is wrong with him? Why does he feel so inadequate that he needs an expensive car to make him feel like a real man?*

Whenever you see a movie that takes place in Hollywood (especially a comedy or parody), the movie industry people (actors, directors, producers) are all driving very expensive cars. The cars say: *Look at me—I am successful. My last movie was a hit.* (But I am still insecure.)

Used cars

For many expensive car brands, such as BMW, Mercedes-Benz, Porsche, the body style does not change every year. Therefore, a two-year-old BMW looks just like a brand-new BMW. Therefore, some people buy a used car for half the price of a new car (and keep it clean, and pretend it's new).

The highway numbering system

American highways are numbered like this: Roads that go east and west are given even numbers (10, 44, 66) and highways that run north and south have odd numbers, 5, 45, 95. The lower the even number, the farther south the road is. For example, Interstate 10 runs from Florida through Louisiana to southern California, and Interstate 94 runs through North Dakota. The lower the odd number, the farther west the highway is. For example, California highway Interstate 5 runs near the Pacific coast. And Interstate 95 runs along the Atlantic coast.

Most major American cities have an interstate highway loop around them. These numbers of these loops have three digits (610), whereas the highway numbers have two digits (20).

BUS LANES

American highways don't have bus lanes, but some have HOV (high-occupancy vehicle) lanes near cities. These lanes are for cars with two or more people and are meant to encourage carpooling. Some cities have begun to offer use of the HOV lanes to cars with only one person, if the person pays a toll. This is called a HOT (high-occupancy toll) lane and is popular because there is less traffic in these lanes.

LISTENING & PRONOUNCING

1. Play the **MODEL CONVERSATION** several times and fill in the blanks.
2. Listen again, pronounce, and record yourself. And listen to yourself.

 45

Britney   Hey, Brad. _____?

Brad   Exhausting. It's ironic. I'm super busy on the weekends, and I _____ during the week.

Britney   _____.

Brad   Enough sarcasm.

Britney   Sorry. So, again, how was your weekend?

Brad   Well, you know I have a _____ with my uncle on Saturdays. I like working for him, but his office is so far away, it takes over an hour by subway to get there.

Britney   Bummer. You commute to school _____ and to work _____.

Brad   Yeah. He's offered to pay for a taxi, but the traffic is _____ in Gangnam, so I wouldn't save any time.

Britney   You ever think of getting a _____?

Brad   My uncle wants me to. I could show American clients around and _____ for them.

Britney   _____. Sounds like you have a future with your uncle's company.

Brad   We'll see. Driving and speaking English—talk about _____!

Britney   You can do it, Brad. _____!

Brad   Thanks.

Britney   You like the guys who work for your uncle?

Brad   Yeah, they're all hard-working _____. Not a _____ in the bunch. Well, his daughter, my first cousin is, well . . . No, this is the new me. I'm not going _____ my boss's daughter.

Britney   Good idea. Is your uncle a nice boss?

Brad   Oh yeah, he's a _____. He's hands-off and doesn't micro-manage.

Britney   Is he a _____?

Brad   Yes, but it's his company. He's an _____ and a self-made man. Say, after you graduate, you might be a good fit for his company.

Britney   _____? Why do you say that?

Brad   You're a _____, and that's one thing his company lacks. Do you plan on following the _____ or the _____?

Britney   I want to follow the _____. I want my own money so I can marry for love, and not for financial security.

Brad   Sounds like you've given it a lot of thought.

Britney   Like you said, I'm a _____.

ARTICLES & PREPOSITIONS

> 1. Fill in the blanks with an **ARTICLE** (*a, an,* or *the*). Some blanks may need no answer.
> 2. Listen to the audio file and check your answers. Then listen again and repeat. 🎧 46

My father is _____ branch manager for _____ Kookmin Bank. He's _____ company man, and he's worked for them for twenty years. He has great loyalty to them. Every now and then, another bank will wine and dine him to try to hire him, but he never leaves. He says _____ banking is easy, people are hard. He's _____ real people person, and _____ big part of his job is keeping the workers happy and their morale up. He remembers when he was _____ low man on the totem pole, so he shows extra attention to _____ new workers.

My mom, on _____ other hand, is _____ entrepreneur. She worked for _____ company for about three years, learned all she could, and then started her own company. Right now, she runs three small companies, and she's working at _____ real-estate office to learn that business. She is definitely on _____ career path. She would be bored staying home and cleaning _____ house.

I've had two part-time jobs in my life. Last summer, I tutored two neighborhood kids in _____ math while they were preparing for _____ university entrance exams. That job was OK, but I spent more time making them behave than I did teaching math. Sometimes I felt like I was just _____ glorified babysitter. But _____ money was good, so what _____ heck. Now I work at _____ a 7-11, and that is low stress. And _____ low pay.

> 3. Fill in the blanks with a **PREPOSITION** or a **DURATION** word. 🎧 43-44
>   AT   ABOUT   FOR   IN   OF   ON   DURING   TO   UNTIL   WHEN
> 4. Listen to the Conversation Starters and check your answers. Then listen and pronounce.

1. 1Q   What about a full-time job _____ the semester break?

2. 2Q   Does he do any work _____ home _____ the weekends?

3. 2A   My father works _____ a bank. Every now and then, he works _____ home.

4. 3Q   Does your mother work? Is she _____ the career track or the mommy track?

5. 4A   I'd like to follow the career track and make money _____ we have a baby, and then work part-time.

6. 7Q   What does your father or mother like most _____ their job?

7. 15A   He goes _____ China once a year.

> **1. Fill in the blanks with a Vocabulary Vitamin from page 74.**
>
> **2. Do the matching.**

1. The traffic was _____. It took us three hours to get across Gangnam.

2. My father is a(n) _____. He takes wedding photos.

3. My brother is a(n) _____. He prefers to work alone and to communicate by email.

4. She's a(n) _____. If she has nothing to do, she'll go help somebody else with their job.

5. He's a(n) _____. He's worked for them for fifteen years.

1	boss from hell	anti-social; hermit	1
2	boss's pet	badmouth	2
3	brownnose	detail person	3
4	goes by the book	disorganized	4
5	career track	entrepreneur	5
6	company man	in the doghouse	6
7	happy camper	loose cannon	7
8	have your act together	low man on the totem pole	8
9	idea person	mommy track	9
10	lone wolf	moody; malcontent	10
11	people person	pushover	11
12	queen bee	slacker	12
13	self-starter	team player	13
14	top dog	watch the clock	14
15	workaholic	worker bee	15

6. I'm a(n) _____. I hate doing detailed work.

7. She's a(n) _____. She's only 30, and she's already started four businesses.

8. What a(n) _____. Look at him, sleeping at his desk. He even brings a pillow.

9. I hate _____ traffic on Friday. It takes an hour longer than usual.

10. I've been working here four years, and I'm still just a(n) _____.

> **3. Go to jazzenglish.com, listen to the short dialogs, and mark the best answer. Sometimes there are two good answers. Choose the best one. Then listen and pronounce.**

	1	2	3	4	5	6	7	8	9	10
A	○	○	○	○	○	○	○	○	○	○
B	○	○	○	○	○	○	○	○	○	○
C	○	○	○	○	○	○	○	○	○	○
D	○	○	○	○	○	○	○	○	○	○

Write your scores here and again on page 58.

Articles	Vocabulary	Total correct
/21	/10	/52
Prepositions	Listening Quiz	% correct
/11	/10	

ACADEMIC CONVERSATIONS

1. **Read the sample answers and write your own. Try to use new vocabulary.**
2. **If you do not like the question, make up your own and answer it.**
3. **Give specific examples: names, dates, times, places, amounts, whatever.**
4. **Why don't you type the answers on a computer and tape them here? That's what A+ students do.**

1. **Are you an idea person or a detail person?**

   I'm definitely an idea person. <u>First</u>, I usually look at the big picture. I'm not too concerned about some details. <u>Second</u>, I'm creative and think outside of the box. I love trying new and better ways to do things. Often while jogging, I have some really great ideas. It must be the adrenaline. <u>Third</u>, I love thinking. Sometimes I think it is important to step back and think about things.

   _____

   _____

   _____

   _____

2. **Are you a team player or a lone wolf?**

   I'm a team player. <u>First</u>, I'm an outgoing person, so I like working with others. <u>Second</u>, I think we can achieve more if we work together. A person working alone is never as effective as a group working together. <u>Third</u>, the lone wolf usually gets killed by the pack. I think it's safer and more productive to be a team player.

   _____

   _____

   _____

   _____

3. **Are you a people person or a shy introvert?**

   <u>It depends</u> on my mood. Usually, I'm a people person. At school, I'm a social butterfly. I belong to many clubs and have many friends. <u>However</u>, sometimes I'm a shy introvert. Occasionally, I like to stay home and recharge my batteries. Some weekends, I turn off my phone and try to read a book. It's ironic: when I have energy, I get energized being around people. But when I'm tired, being around people tires me out.

   _____

   _____

   _____

   _____

SPECIFIC EXAMPLES

Because	For example	For instance	Also	Finally
Half and half.	It depends.	On the other hand	However	

4. Is your father an entrepreneur or a company man?

My father is a company man. He's worked for the same company for the past twenty years. He says that working in a company is safer and less stressful. <u>However</u>, he told me that when he retires he wants to open up his own business. I guess years of working at the same company for years has inspired him to become an entrepreneur.

_____

_____

_____

_____

5. Will you follow the career track or the mommy track? Do you want your wife to follow . . .?

In a perfect world, I would like my wife to follow the career track until we have our first baby, and then quit work. Then after our children are in school, she would go back to work again—maybe as a freelance or self-employed. I think it's important for the mom to be there all the time when a baby is young. <u>On the other hand</u>, if we have no children, I hope my wife becomes a CEO.

_____

_____

_____

_____

6. Are you a self-starter or do you watch the clock? Are you a self-starter or a slacker?

I'm a slacker. <u>First</u>, ... Hey, I AM a slacker. I'm too lazy to list three reasons.

No, wait. I can do this. I'm a slacker because <u>first</u>, my pen is too heavy. My hand gets tired. <u>Second</u>, my pen ran out of ink. <u>Third</u>, I can't find any paper. Whoa. This answer exhausted me.

_____

_____

_____

_____

ANSWER KEY

1 All About Me

1. night owl
2. couch potato
3. short fuse
4. neat freak
5. gullible
6. party pooper
7. attention span
8. procrastinate
9. loner
10. stuck-up

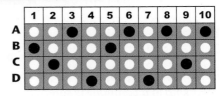

Vocabulary Workout Answers

	1	2	3	4	5	6	7	8	9	10
A	○	●	○	●	○	●	○	●	○	●
B	●	○	○	○	○	●	○	○	○	○
C	○	●	○	○	○	○	○	●	○	○
D	○	○	○	●	○	○	●	○	○	○

To check the matching answers,
open your student book to page 18.

2 Weekends & Neighborhoods

1. quality time
2. hang out
3. sick and tired
4. recharged my batteries
5. catch up on
6. tentative plans
7. got the blues
8. pout
9. weekend warrior
10. burned out / drained

	1	2	3	4	5	6	7	8	9	10
A	●	○	○	○	○	○	○	●	○	○
B	○	○	●	○	○	●	○	○	○	○
C	○	●	○	○	○	○	●	○	○	○
D	○	○	○	●	○	○	○	○	○	●

3 Technology

1. big spender
2. memory stick, memory card
3. virus, spam
4. instant gratification
5. skeptical
6. impulse buyer
7. search engine
8. apps
9. frugal
10. Photoshop

	1	2	3	4	5	6	7	8	9	10
A	●	○	○	●	○	●	○	○	○	●
B	○	●	○	○	○	○	○	●	○	○
C	○	○	○	●	○	○	●	○	●	○
D	○	○	●	○	○	○	○	○	○	○

4 Dating & Nightlife

1. admired her from afar
2. stood me up
3. puppy love
4. two-timer
5. love at first sight
6. Dear John letter
7. crushed
8. wet blanket
9. the silent treatment
10. cheap drunk

	1	2	3	4	5	6	7	8	9	10
A	○	○	○	●	●	○	○	○	○	○
B	○	●	○	○	○	○	●	○	○	●
C	●	○	○	○	○	○	○	●	○	○
D	○	○	●	○	○	●	○	●	○	○

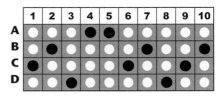

To check the matching answers,
open your student book to page 42.

ANSWER KEY

5 Sofa Time: TV, Music, & Reading

1. bloopers
2. plot twist
3. sequel
4. prime time
5. Cinderella
6. girl-next-door type, *femme fatale*
7. ensemble cast
8. sidekick
9. chemistry
10. soap opera

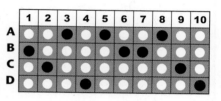

6 Health & Fitness

1. ache, black and blue / bruised
2. sore
3. rash
4. dizzy
5. swollen, sprain
6. pollen, sinuses
7. cold turkey
8. nauseous
9. pimple
10. rehab

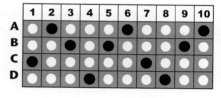

7 Holidays, Festivals, & Feelings

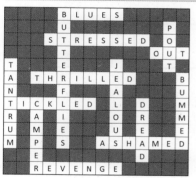

1. sick and tired
2. temper tantrum
3. soothing
4. Yuck / Gross
5. pout
6. embarrassed / ashamed
7. envious, jealous / jealous, envious
8. furious, revenge
9. anxious
10. monotonous / tedious

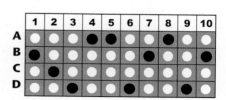

8 Working & Getting There

1. bumper-to-bumper
2. freelance
3. lone wolf
4. self-starter
5. company man
6. idea person
7. entrepreneur
8. slacker
9. rush hour
10. gofer / grunt

To check the matching answers,
open your student book to page 74.

UNIT SCORES

Unit	Articles	Prepositions	Vocabulary	Listening	% correct	How long did it take you?
1						
2						
3						
4						
5						
6						
7						
8						

Average scores
